From their operations in the redemp[tion] interaction in the lives of human be[ings] fascination in the hearts and minds of believers throughout church history. However, over the past century, this captivation with the angelic world has grown cold. In this new primer, Tim Chester answers common questions and helps reawaken our interest in this vast multitude of God's creation.

Dustin Benge
Associate Professor of Biblical Spirituality and Historical Theology,
The Southern Baptist Theological Seminary, Louisville, Kentucky

For many people, talk of supernatural powers – heavenly beings, spirits, Satan and angels – either raises a quizzical eyebrow or creates a fog of bewilderment. In this illuminating and enthralling book, Tim Chester ranges across scripture to explain this apparently mysterious spiritual realm with remarkable clarity and simplicity, and shows us how understanding the nature and role of angels will impact our worship, our emotions, our prayers and our devotion to the Lord Jesus and His gospel. A wonderful biblical overview which opens our eyes to profound truth.

Jonathan Lamb
Author, teacher and minister-at-large, Keswick Ministries

People are fascinated by angels. Unfortunately, much popular Christian literature, not to mention non-Christian media, gives scant attention to the actual biblical data about angels. With brevity and faithfulness, Tim Chester guides us to a deeper understanding of these 'ministering spirits who are sent to serve those who will inherit salvation' (Heb. 1:14).

Robert L. Plummer
Collin and Evelyn Aikman Professor of Biblical Studies,
The Southern Baptist Theological Seminary, Louisville, Kentucky

ANGELS

WHEN HEAVEN MEETS EARTH

TIM CHESTER

CHRISTIAN
FOCUS

Copyright © Tim Chester 2022
paperback ISBN 978-1-5271-0886-8
ebook ISBN 978-1-5271-0924-7

First published in 2022
by
Christian Focus Publications Ltd,
Geanies House, Fearn, Ross-shire
IV20 1TW, Scotland
www.christianfocus.com

Cover design by MOOSE77

Printed and bound by
Bell & Bain, Glasgow

MIX
Paper from
responsible sources
FSC
www.fsc.org
FSC® C007785

Contents

Introduction

Nearly eight in ten Americans believe in angels. Even among those who never attend church it's four out of ten.[1] In the United Kingdom one in three people believe they have a guardian angel.[2] You may well be one of them. Every tenth person in your street or workplace thinks they may have seen or heard an angel in some way. Again, you may be one of them. Books telling the story of angelic encounters are best-

---

1. 'Nearly 8 in 10 Americans Believe in Angels'. CBS News, 23 December 2011, https://www.cbsnews.com/news/poll-nearly-8-in-10-americans-believe-in-angels/; accessed 8 September, 2021.

2. The Bible Society, 'A Third of All Brits Believe in Guardian Angels', 13 December 2016, https://www.biblesociety.org.uk/latest/news/a-third-of-all-brits-believe-in-guardian-angels/; accessed 30 August, 2021.

sellers. Despite the widespread rejection of Christianity in our culture, many people are still fascinated by angels.

But what we can know for sure about angels? Are we dependent on second-hand accounts? Are we left with conjecture and guess work? This book goes back to the most reliable source we have for information about angels – God Himself speaking through the Bible.

1.

The Mysterious World of Angels

A few years ago my parents told me a story involving the granddaughter of old family friends. Her name is Bethany. In 2016 Bethany was heading off on holiday with a friend called Natasha, accompanied by Natasha's Dad. Bethany and Natasha were fifteen, and both were Christians.

On the flight, Natasha felt unwell and found she had red welts on her skin. Then she said, 'Daddy, help me, I can't breathe.' She lost consciousness and went into cardiac arrest. She was having an allergic reaction to sesame seeds in a baguette she had bought in the airport. She knew she had an allergy, but the packaging hadn't mentioned the sesame seeds. You may have heard about the story in the news. It led to new regulations on food labelling in the UK known as 'Natasha's Law'.

Natasha was carried into the cockpit where her father twice tried to revive her with an EpiPen. Once the plane landed, paramedics administered CPR. They used such force in their desperation that they broke her ribs. Suddenly Natasha's father turned to Bethany and said, 'What are those angels doing?' Bethany said, 'I can't see any angels.' 'They're taking my daughter away,' said Natasha's father. The following day Natasha's life support machine was switched off.

After Natasha's death, her mother, then her brother and finally her father, all became Christians. In a subsequent interview, Natasha's father, Nadim Ednan-Laperouse, described seeing an intense light from which five winged-figures appeared. He told the BBC: 'They were about twenty centimetres tall, not chubby like children in a Renaissance painting or with feathery wings like in the Vatican, but actually like human beings, all looking at me, moving around Natasha. I'd never ever seen anything like that in my life.' He tried to wave them away, shouting 'This is not her time.' The figures disappeared. That was the moment Natasha died.

At the time, Ednan-Laperouse was an atheist. The founder of the Wow Toys company, he had been awarded an MBE by the Queen for his services to business. His experience as an entrepreneur had taught him to be calm in a crisis. 'I am the least likely person to have an hallucination,' he comments. 'I am not prone to such things ever ... To those who say, "I don't believe you," I say, "What have I to gain by making this up?" I don't mind if people think I am a fool, but I know it is the truth. No one can tell me I did not see that.'[1]

---

1. 'A Bright Yellow Light', BBC, https://www.bbc.co.uk/programmes/articles/1c575Zkjg7RDmy3Hgd0lKrP/a-bright-yellow-light; accessed 28 August, 2021.

In 1975 five years of bloody civil war in Cambodia came to an end when the communist Khmer Rouge took control of the capital, Phnom Penh. What followed was a four-year reign of terror in which Cambodia became 'the first country to be transformed into a concentration camp in its entirety'.[2] The population were forced from towns and cities to work in the fields. Intellectuals were massacred, technologies were destroyed, and thousands starved as the country was transformed into a peasant economy. In total around two million people died – more than a quarter of the population. Ninety per cent of Christians were martyred. Yet, amidst the chaos, God also protected some in the mystery of His providence.

Pastor Reach Yeah, a former president of the Cambodian Evangelical Church, was forced to leave Phnom Penh along with everyone else. He found himself in a remote location where he was given a job herding cows and buffaloes. But he and his family escaped the worst excesses of the new regime. Somehow they lived in relative peace.

> From time to time passers-by would surprise Pastor Yeah by enquiring, 'Who is that stranger who comes and goes and sits on the steps of your house?' At first, Yeah was puzzled by this, for he was aware of no friend whom he had entertained or who might linger at the door of his house. But as the gossip persisted, Yeah came to understand who the stranger was, even though his own eyes were never opened to see him … That simple thatch hut, on the edge of the commune, stood on

---

2. Bernard Levin, The Times, 22 April, 1976; cited in Don Cormack, *Killing Fields, Living Fields*, (MARC OMF), 179.

sacred ground. It was visited with angelic protection, and no-one dared violate it.[3]

In late 1974 and early 1975 a number of women were sexually assaulted in Cambridge by a man whom the press dubbed 'the Cambridge Rapist'. He wore a crudely-stitched leather mask with the word 'rapist' across the forehead. After a massive manhunt, the police arrested a man named Peter Cook who was sentenced to life in prison for a total of nine offences. Another victim had successfully managed to fight him off when he tried to force his way into her flat.

While Cook was still at large, a young Christian woman was walking home at night when she became aware that she was being followed by a hooded man. Suddenly another man appeared and walked alongside her without saying a word. He walked with her all the way to her front door and then vanished into the night.[4]

During the 1960s Martinho Campos was a leader in the church in Mozambique. At one point, while leading a series of meetings away from his home region, he was arrested. The local police chief, a European, assumed the meetings were associated with Frelimo freedom fighters. So Campos was arrested and jailed without trial. An intervention by the local Catholic priest failed to secure his release. The police chief was not going to let a concern for justice get in the way of maintaining order. Then one night the police chief was conveying a group of prisoners in a truck when

3. Don Cormack, *Killing Fields, Living Fields*, (MARC OMF), 199.

4. This story was told to me by Peter Comont, Senior Pastor of Trinity Church Oxford and a former pastor in Cambridge.

he saw 'what appeared to be a man in gleaming white, standing in the road, facing him'. He swerved sharply to avoid the man and rolled the truck. He was trapped underneath and was only released by the prisoners collectively lifting the truck from him.

After his release from hospital, the police chief went straight to Campos to ask for forgiveness. Campos told him of his need for God's forgiveness and explained how he could be forgiven through faith in Christ. The police chief asked Campos to pray for him and then called for hot water so Campos could wash. A fair trial was arranged and Campos was soon released. But not only was he released, the police chief also gave him official permission to travel throughout the region.[5]

Dr Otto Piper was the Professor of New Testament Literature and Exegesis at Princeton Theological Seminary in the 1940s and 1950s. He grew up in Germany, but in 1933 he was expelled by the Nazis. He arrived at Liverpool Street station in central London without knowing anyone and having no idea where he should go. As he went out into the street a well-dressed gentleman came up to him. In a Scottish accent the man said, 'Professor Piper, come with me.' Professor Piper had never seen the man before. But, with no other options, he chose to follow him. The man took him to a boarding house and arranged for him to have a room. When Professor Piper turned to thank the man, he had gone.[6]

---

5. Phyllis Thompson, *Life Out of Death in Mozambique*, (Hodder & Stoughton, 1989), 111; cited in John Piper, *Let the Nations Be Glad*, (IVP, 2nd Ed., 2003), 99-100.

6. Joe Martin, 'Genesis 18: Abraham's Prayer', sermon at St Ebbes, Oxford, 28 January 2009, https://www.crosspreach.com/series/1624/abraham_father_of_us_all; accessed 3 April 2021.

Chrissie Chapman arrived in Burundi in the 1980s to open a maternity clinic serving the needs of 72,000 people. She went from working in a large London hospital where doctors were always on hand, to working in a building that not only had no doctors, but no running water. In October 1993 the elected president was assassinated in a failed military coup, and Chrissie found herself in the midst of what would prove to be a thirteen-year-long genocidal civil war. She was forced to evacuate the clinic so she started working in camps for displaced people. One night a local pastor called on her: a mother in the camps had died, leaving a baby; could Chrissie help? Five days later Chrissie had seventeen babies on bean bags in her living room. Within a few months she had over fifty children. As she says, with a twinkle in her eye, 'I'm single, I have no husband and I have fifty-four children, all with different fathers.'[7]

One evening Chrissie was sitting on the doorstep of her mud hut with a colleague named David. Around them they could hear the sound of gunfire and terrified screams. Together they prayed for peace and protection. Suddenly David stood up and began to praise God, 'Thank you, Jesus; thank you, Jesus.' Turning to Chrissie, he said, 'Chrissie, just look at the walls.' Chrissie could see nothing. So David knelt down, touched her eyes and prayed that God would open her eyes. 'As I opened my eyes,' writes Chrissie, 'I saw dozens of huge angels standing shoulder to shoulder on top of the six-foot high wall that surrounded the perimeter of our healing centre.' Chrissie describes them as 'clothed in full armour'. They stood with their back to Chrissie

---

7. Westmont College, 'Chapel: Chrissie Chapman, 14 November, 2016', https://youtu.be/GFfFBS69rM8; accessed 29 March, 2021.

and David, facing out towards the darkness. 'I was filled with so much awe,' she writes, 'that every bit of fear drained out of my body and could no longer touch me.'[8]

Paul Barnett is a respected academic and was, until his retirement, the bishop of North Sydney. He is currently a fellow in ancient history at Macquarie University, Australia, and research professor at Regent College, Canada. In 2019 he was made a member of the Order of Australia by the Queen.

Barnett tells the story of going out on a 'surftie', a cross between a surfboard and kayak. The idea is that you crash out through the waves before turning your surftie round and riding a wave back into the shore. During the first couple of days of their family holiday the sea had been too rough for surfing. But on day three bravado got the better of Barnett and he set out into the sea. He managed to plough through the water and experienced the thrill of surfing a wave back towards the shore. So out he went again. For an hour everything was great. But by this point the tide and wind had changed. Suddenly he was confronted by a huge wave. As it crashed over him, it wrenched the surftie and paddle from his hands. He was left adrift. There was nobody else around: he was on his own, about a quarter of a mile from the shore. Caught by an undertow, he found himself being carried out to sea. And all the time huge waves continued to crash over him. 'This is it,' he thought. 'I made my peace once more with the Lord,' he recalled. 'I really did not expect to see my wife again.'

Suddenly, out of nowhere a man Barnett describes as an 'ocker', an uncultured character, appeared in a faded green wet suit sitting

---

8. Chrissie Chapman, *The Night the Angels Came: Miracles Of Protection And Provision In Burundi*, (Monarch, 2016), 37.

upon a surf kayak. 'You're in a spot of trouble, old pal, aren't you?' he said. 'I've never done this before,' he went on, 'but I think I can get you in.' As a large wave approached, he told Barnett to wrap his arms round his stomach. The wave drove them towards the shore before crashing over them. But they emerged from the white water and the man paddled to within fifty yards of the shore. 'You can drop off here, mate,' he said, and Barnett crawled back onto the beach. 'I didn't believe in angels much before,' says Barnett, 'but I tell you I had never seen him before and I've never seen him since. And I'm sure he wasn't out there when I was there. He just appeared.'[9]

Many angel stories can feel a little bit like urban myths: they involve an unnamed friend of a friend, and often conform to typical patterns with only incidental details changed. And perhaps many of them are myths – stories that have grown and expanded each time they have been passed on. But other stories are told by named people about their own experiences. They include people with no obvious predisposition to gullibility. Some, like the business people and academics I've named, have a vested interest in appearing intellectually aloof from anything as apparently fanciful as angels.

So what are we to make of these stories?

There are reasons to be cautious when we hear tales of the supernatural. One reason is that some people are charlatans.

---

9. Paul Barnett, 'Evangelism that is Apostolic Part 1,' Evangelical Ministry Assembly 1992, Proclamation Trust, http://www.proctrust.org.uk/resources/talk/539. Accessed 29 March 2021.

The sad reality is that where there is money to be made people will spin a yarn for a profit. Many people long to be reassured by the idea that they have a guardian angel and other people are willing to exploit that longing. Not for a minute should we assume every angel story is being peddled by a charlatan. But some are and so some caution is appropriate.

A second reason to be cautious is that the Bible says, 'Satan himself masquerades as an angel of light' (2 Cor. 11:14). Not every supernatural encounter is benign. Don't be so keen for some kind of experience of transcendence or power that you are deceived by Satan. In the popular imagination Satan is an obviously impish figure with horns and a tail. But, when it suits his purposes, he can appear plausible and attractive.

Third, people may misinterpret what has happened to them. They may genuinely experience something and they may have no intention of deceiving anyone. But how we interpret an event is shaped by our presuppositions and expectations. Suppose you see a light in the sky. If you're a firm believer in UFOs then you might readily conclude you've seen signs of extra-terrestrial life. But if you're a UFO-sceptic then you'll probably put it down to a passing aircraft. Two people might see the same thing and come to different conclusions or describe it in different terms. This means experience alone is an unreliable guide and it means experience is not the same as interpretation. Someone may present a sincere account of a genuine experience, but that doesn't guarantee that their interpretation of that experience is accurate.

This means we need a reliable framework to understand our experiences. Fortunately God has not left us in the dark. He's told us everything we need to know to make sense of life – and that includes angels. So we're going to look at what the Bible says about angels.

And the first thing to say is that angels are real. While it may be right to exercise some caution, that doesn't mean we need be completely sceptical. Just because some accounts of angels are suspect doesn't mean we must reject every account. The story of the Bible clearly demonstrates that angels exist and that they are sometimes involved in the lives of human beings.

Many hundreds of years before the coming of Jesus, during a period when God's people were oppressed by a foreign nation, an angel appeared to a husband and wife. The angel came first to the woman. She was barren, but the angel promised that she would have a child, a child who would deliver Israel from their oppression. She told her husband, 'A man of God came to me. He looked like an angel of God, very awesome. I didn't ask him where he came from, and he didn't tell me his name' (Judg. 13:6). Her husband, who was named Manoah, then prayed that God would send 'the man of God' a second time to teach them how to raise this special child. So again the angel came to the woman. This time she hurried to fetch her husband. Manoah invited the man to stay for a meal, not yet realising it was an angel. When Manoah asked his name, the angel replied, 'Why do you ask my name? It is beyond understanding' (Judg. 13:18). It could also be translated, 'My name is wonderful.'

The angel invited Manoah to make a sacrificial offering to God. The Bible then says, 'the LORD did an amazing thing while Manoah and his wife watched' (Judg. 13:19). The angel stepped into the flame and ascended into heaven. At this the two of them fell to the ground – they realised they had met an angel. 'We are doomed to die!' said Manoah. 'We have seen God' (Judg. 13:22). But his wife pointed out that if God had intended to kill them He wouldn't have accepted their offering, nor told them of His plans for them. Their child was Samson, the famously strong man who battled against the oppressors of God's people, as the angel had promised.

All successful military campaigns rely on good intelligence along with the ability to keep the enemy in the dark. Once, when the nation of Aram was at war with Israel, the prophet Elisha kept providing divinely-gifted military intelligence to the Israelite king. 'Beware of passing that place,' he would say, 'because the Arameans are going down there.' 'Time and again,' we're told, 'Elisha warned the king, so that he was on his guard in such places' (2 Kings 6:9-10). At first the King of Aram thought he had a traitor among his ranks, but eventually he realised that the 'intel' came from Elisha. So he immediately ordered Elisha's capture. His troops surrounded the city where Elisha was staying with 'horses and chariots and a strong force' (2 Kings 6:14). Elisha's servant was thrown into a panic. 'Oh no, my lord!' he cried. 'What shall we do?' (2 Kings 6:15).

> 'Don't be afraid,' the prophet answered. 'Those who are with us are more than those who are with them.' And Elisha prayed, 'Open his eyes, Lord, so that he may see.' Then the Lord opened the servant's eyes, and he looked and saw the hills full of horses and chariots of fire all around Elisha (2 Kings 6:16-17).

The servant was enabled to see an army of angels. They were there all the time, hidden from human sight. Only in answer to prayer was the servant able to see them. I suspect angels are present to protect God's people many more times than we realise. Often we may not even be aware of their intervention as they head off danger before it even arrives. In the story of Elisha the angelic army temporarily blinds the Aramean soldiers. Elisha then led them to the Israelite capital. When their eyes were finally opened they found themselves right in the heart of the enemy camp. In a lovely twist, the king of Israel prepared a feast for them before sending them home. That must have been an interesting occasion with POWs finding themselves dining at enemy expense. It did the trick because the nation of Aram stopped sending raiding parties into Israelite territory.

In the early days of the church the Apostle Peter was imprisoned by King Herod. This was no small matter since Herod had just executed Peter's fellow apostle, James. So the church gathered to pray for Peter. As was common in the Roman world, Peter was chained to two soldiers to prevent any possibility of escape. During the night 'an angel of the Lord appeared and a light shone in the cell' (Acts 12:7). The angel struck Peter to wake him. 'Quick, get up!' he said (Acts 12:7). As Peter did so, the chains fell away from his wrists. The angel told Peter to put on his sandals and cloak. Then he followed the angel out of the prison. 'Peter … had no idea that what the angel was doing was really happening; he thought he was seeing a vision' (Acts 12:9). As they passed the guards, the guards ignored them. As they approached the prison doors, the doors swung open of their own accord. After leading Peter one block away from the prison, the angel disappeared. Only then did Peter realise this was for real.

Then the story takes a somewhat comedic turn. Peter arrived at the house where the church had gathered to pray for his release. His knock on the door was answered by a servant girl called Rhoda. Recognising Peter's voice, she rushed back to tell everyone else. In her excitement she neglected to let Peter in. 'Peter is at the door!' she exclaimed. But no one believed her. '"You're out of your mind," they told her. When she kept insisting that it was so, they said, "It must be his angel"' (Acts 12:14-15). Meanwhile Peter was still knocking on the door, presumably wondering what was going on inside. They were praying for Peter to be released, but didn't believe it when God answered their prayer.

Perhaps you assume people in Bible times were more gullible than people today. In fact there were sceptics then just as there are now. The Bible itself records: 'The Sadducees say that there is no resurrection, and that there are neither angels nor spirits, but the Pharisees believe all these things' (Acts 23:8). The Sadducees were a faction drawn from the elite of first-century Judaism. The point is there were plenty of people around who did not believe in angels. Even those who believed in angels in theory sometimes had a hard time believing it when angels actually turned up – like the Apostle Peter who, as we've just seen, assumed his angelic deliverer was just a vision. So when people believed in angelic activity it wasn't simply because everyone did. It wasn't unthinking or unquestioning belief. They had the option (along with the Sadducees) to reject the claims of those who said they had encountered angels. But the first Christians believed in angels because they found the accounts credible or because they had their own direct experience.

ANGELS REMIND US THAT THERE'S
MORE TO LIFE THAN STUFF

An interest in angels has not gone away. A quick look in a bookshop reveals the on-going fascination people have with angels. In *Angels in My Hair*, the best-selling autobiography of Lorna Byrne, Byrne claims: 'I see angels all the time I'm awake.' 'Their wings,' she says elsewhere, 'are beautiful beyond words.' *Angel Whispers* by Jenny Smedley, who lives in Somerset with her reincarnated dog, identifies four key levels of angels beginning with 'odd job angels' who get us parking spaces and find lost keys. Angels are normally unseen, she tells us, 'except perhaps as the little black dots that you sometimes see zipping across the room out of the corner of your eye.' In *The Miracles of Archangel Michael*, Doreen Virtue purports to tell us how to access the help of angels. Basically we just need to ask, she claims. But some things help like putting lots of greenery in our homes. 'Plants,' she explains, 'absorb the energy of our fear and stress the same way that they absorb carbon dioxide.'[10] (Doreen Virtue has subsequently renounced her old views about angels after becoming a Christian in 2017.)[11]

Some of this fascination with angels may be a bit muddled at times. But it reflects an important intuition. Angels are important. Let me suggest a couple of reasons why it's good to think about angels.

---

10. James Walton, 'We Believe in Angels', The Spectator, 24 February 2010, https://www.spectator.co.uk/2010/02/we-believe-in-angels. Accessed 30 August, 2021.

11. See doreenvirtue.com and Doreen Virtue, *Deceived No More; How Jesus Led Me Out of the New Age and Into His Word* (Thomas Nelson, 2020).

One of the appeals of angels is the very fact that they're weird. They're not part of our normal experience. They remind us that there's more to life than stuff.

A key feature of our dominant worldview, at least in the Western world, is materialism. There's a philosophical version of this which says that reality only consists of what can be touched and seen. The world is stuff made of atoms and nothing else. There's nothing beyond the edge of the universe. In the end even human beings are just the molecules in our bodies. Our 'self' is no more than the sum total of the neural connections in our brain.

There's a more practical version of materialism as well. This assumes the main aim in life is to get stuff – more money, a bigger house, the latest fashions, a flashy car, the new gadget. Stuff is what makes us happy. It's a view peddled by a thousand adverts. Buy this dress and you'll be loved. Buy this car and you'll be happy. Go on holiday and discover your true self.

But many people rightly suspect there's more to life than stuff. Perhaps they have a philosophy; perhaps it's just an intuition. But they suspect people are more than the molecules in their brains and certainly more than the stuff in their closets. And an interest in angels is one sign of this. Angels are a reminder that there's more to life than what we can see.

ANGELS REMIND US THAT WE NEED SOMEONE TO LOOK AFTER US

Another reason people are attracted to angels is that we want someone to look after us. Angels are often portrayed in our culture as caring and protective. There's a common belief that people have a guardian angel, a personal angelic protector.

And we find that comforting because for most of us life feels precarious.

We worry about whether our health might fail, or whether a friend might betray us, or whether we might lose our job, or whether we might become a victim of crime. We do our best to ensure that we, and those we love, are safe. Human beings like to think we are conquering the planet, taming the wilderness, overcoming disease. When an accident occurs there's a public outcry. The assumption is that every accident is preventable. If someone had done their job properly, or if the appropriate regulations had been in place, then this could have been averted. Sometimes that's right – we do have a duty of care towards those around us. But perhaps we also recognise there's a limit to human power. Not every accident can be prevented. Not every concern can be allayed. We can't protect ourselves from every eventuality. Human beings are finite. We are vulnerable.

So the thought that supernatural beings might be present to provide an extra layer of protection is very attractive. Angels remind us that we need someone to look after us.

But should we look to angels for protection? What are angels actually like and what do they do?

2.

What are Angels?

Christmas cards seem to be on the way out. As fewer people send written letters through the post, so fewer people are sending physical Christmas cards. My daughters look scornfully at us when we ask if they plan to send any greetings cards. The WhatsApp generation is content to exchange messages and memes on Christmas morning.

Perhaps the demise of Christmas cards will lead to the demise of the strange, sanitised version of angels they typically depict. Christmas-card angels seems to be either slender human figures wearing head-to-toe robes or chubby babies floating around like hovering bees. Is this what angels are like?

ANGELS ARE SPIRITS

The Bible says angels are 'spirits' (Heb. 1:14). That doesn't actually tell us very much because it quickly takes us into territory beyond our experience. Human beings also have spiritual souls, but our souls are combined with physical bodies, and we find it all but impossible to conceive of a being without a body. Angels may appear with legs and arms, but this is so we can see them and interact with them. For angels this is only a temporary form and not part of their essential nature. But to say angels don't have bodies is only really to say what is not true of them. It doesn't actually tell us much about what they are. We can't stick an angel under an X-ray machine or in an MRI scanner to discover their chemical composition. The early church father John of Damascus says they are not 'extended in three dimensions'.[1] It might help to think of them as made of pure energy—a kind of celestial force field—rather than physical matter, though even this is probably an analogy at best.

Because angels don't have bodies we can't normally see them unless God specifically enables this. The prophet Balaam was on a mission for the Moabite king which God had told him not to undertake. So en route Balaam's way was blocked by an angel (Num. 22). Balaam himself couldn't see it, but his donkey could and turned off the path to avoid the angel. As this kept happening, Balaam grew increasingly irate and beat the donkey. Eventually we're told 'the LORD opened the donkey's mouth' who then berated Balaam for his cruelty. Finally, God also opened Balaam's eyes so he could see the angel (Num. 22:28, 31). The angel was invisible to Balaam until it was supernaturally revealed to him. The sixteenth-century Reformer John Calvin concludes: 'The angels, to whom is committed the

---

1. John of Damascus, *Exposition of the Orthodox Faith*, 2.3, in *The Nicene and Post-Nicene Fathers: Second Series*, Volume 2, eds. Philip Schaff & Henry Wace, 1899, (reproduced Hendrickson, 1994), 19.

guardianship of the human race, while strenuously applying themselves to their office, yet do not communicate with us in such a way that we become conscious of their presence.'[2] In other words, most of the time we don't realise when angels are at work around us.

The fact that angels don't have bodies also means that, though angels sometimes appear as winged creatures, wings are not an inherent part of their being. Their wings probably represent a much greater ability to move between points in space than is enjoyed by human beings.

ANGELS ARE CREATED

God is eternal. He has always existed. While angels are like God in the sense that both angels and God are spirits, angels are in a completely different category from God. God is the Creator; angels are creatures. There was a time when angels did not exist and they now exist only because God brought them into being. In Colossians 1:15-16 Paul writes:

> The Son is the image of the invisible God, the firstborn over all creation. For in him all things were created: things in heaven and on earth, visible and invisible, whether thrones or powers or rulers or authorities; all things have been created through him and for him.

'All things' includes angels and to drive home the point Paul adds, 'things in heaven and on earth, visible and invisible'. Everything in the heavenly realms apart from God Himself was created by God. Moreover the 'thrones or powers or rulers or authorities' includes spiritual forces, both angels and demons.

---

2. John Calvin, *Genesis*, 1554, trans. John King, (Banner of Truth, 1965), 113.

Angels were created by God and so they are not divine. This means we are not to worship angels or pray to them. We don't seek assistance from angels. Instead, we seek assistance from God through prayer. Maybe He will answer our prayer by sending an angel; maybe He will help us through the kindness of another human being; maybe He will intervene directly. It doesn't really matter what means He uses. The key is that we seek help from God and we give thanks to Him when help comes.

Suppose you're going on a journey. Should you pray to be protected by angels? There's no need. Pray to God for His protection. Perhaps He'll protect you by keeping you awake at the wheel or perhaps by sending an angel at a crucial moment. In one sense it doesn't matter: either way it's God who protects you. Perhaps you'll be aware of an angelic intervention or perhaps you won't. Again, it doesn't matter: either way it's God who protects you. Or perhaps God won't protect you, at least not in the way you envisage. But even if He allows you to have an accident you can be sure He's working for the good of those who love Him. Perhaps He'll use your accident to make you more like Jesus, thereby protecting you from spiritual harm.

ANGELS ARE PERSONAL

Just because angels don't have bodies, we mustn't think of them as impersonal forces. They're personal beings with moral agency.

In the Christmas story, an angel appears to a man called Zechariah to tell him that his wife Elizabeth is going to have a child. The child who is born to them is John the Baptist, the prophet who prepared the way for the coming of Jesus. But when Zechariah first heard this message he was sceptical because Elizabeth had always been barren and now she was too old to have a child. So 'Zechariah asked the angel, "How can I be sure of this? I am an old man and my wife is well along in years"' (Luke 1:18). In response the angel says: 'I am Gabriel. I stand in the presence of God, and I have been sent to speak to you and to tell you this good news' (Luke 1:19).

Notice that angels have personal names. This angel is called 'Gabriel'. Notice too that, though angels act at God's bidding (Gabriel has been sent by God with a message from God), they act with personal agency as beings who can be sent and who can obey. 'Humankind and angel-kind are members of the realm of the personal,' says theologian Graham Cole. 'Both can self-consciously say "I".'[3] Angels are not an amorphous mass of spiritual energy, nor are they mere robots without personality. Indeed, it's hard not to avoid the impression that Gabriel is affronted by Zechariah's scepticism. 'Don't you realise who I am?' he seems to imply. 'Don't you realise I stand in the presence of the Lord? I know what I'm talking about! I'm not making this up. I speak with divine authority.' It's the response of a personal being.

ANGELS ARE POWERFUL

Angels are called 'mighty ones' (Ps. 103:20) and described as 'powerful' (2 Thess. 1:7). As created beings they are lesser than God. Nevertheless, they have a power that exceeds that of human beings (Ps. 8:5). 'They are stronger and more powerful,' says 2 Peter 2:11. Angels are sometimes called 'sons of God' (Job 1:6; 2:1; 38:7 ESV). In Hebrew the phrase 'sons of' doesn't necessarily refer to a descendent – the angels are not God's offspring. Colloquially 'son of' can mean 'sharing

---

3. Graham A. Cole, *Against the Darkness*, (Crossway, 2019), 26.

the characteristics of'. So the disciples James and John were nicknamed 'sons of thunder' because they were short-tempered (Mark 3:17). Angels are called 'sons of God' because, from a human perspective, they share something of the power of God. So Wilhelmus à Brakel, the seventeenth-century Dutch theologian, defines an angel as 'an incorporeal [without a body], personal being which God has created and gifted with an extraordinary intellect, will, and power.'[4]

It's striking that almost every time angels appear to people in the Bible those people fall down in terror. Often the first words an angel says are, 'Do not be afraid.' The reason is clear: when people see an angel their first reaction is fear. Many contemporary accounts of meeting angels are strangely tame compared to the reality presented in the Bible. The word 'cherub' has come to be associated with cute and chubby – the very opposite of the cherubim in the Bible. Angels are frightening!

ANGELS ARE ASEXUAL

As beings without bodies, angels are asexual. On one occasion the Sadducees came to Jesus with a question which they thought would expose the flaws in His theology. The Sadducees didn't believe in a resurrection. So they ask Jesus about a hypothetical woman whose first husband dies. She remarries his brother, but the brother dies. She ends up marrying a total of seven brothers. So whose wife will she be after the resurrection? Jesus began His response by addressing the general issue of resurrection: 'You are in error because you do not know the Scriptures or the power of God.' In other words, there are clear signs of resurrection in the Old Testament Scriptures; besides which we

---

4. Wilhelmus à Brakel, *The Christian's Reasonable Service, Volume One,* (Reformation Heritage Books, 1992), 287.

shouldn't doubt that God has the power to raise people from the dead. Then Jesus addressed their scenario: 'At the resurrection people will neither marry nor be given in marriage; they will be like the angels in heaven' (Matt. 22:29-30). Their scenario was irrelevant because people won't live as married couples at the resurrection. Resurrected human beings will function as angels have always functioned: without marriage and without sex. Or rather all marriage and sexuality will find its fulfilment in the ecstasy and intimacy of the marriage-like relationship between Christ and His people.

The two angels named in the Bible are called 'Gabriel' and 'Michael', and it's easy for us to think of them as male. But the names 'Gabriel' and 'Michael' were not boys' names applied to angels, but angelic names which have subsequently been used for people. Moreover, both names have female versions like 'Gabrielle' and 'Michelle'. There is nothing in the Bible to suggest angels are gendered.

ANGELS ARE SERVANTS OF GOD
Gabriel's interaction with Zechariah also shows us that angels are servants of God. Gabriel doesn't come to Zechariah on his own account. He is sent by God with a message from God. Angels have moral agency, but they don't act independently of God. The psalmist sings:

Praise the Lord, you his angels,
   you mighty ones who do his bidding,
   who obey his word.
Praise the Lord, all his heavenly hosts,
you his servants who do his will (Ps. 103:20-21).

Angels act at God's bidding and obey His commands. This means every angelic message is a message from God and every angelic mission is a mission of God.

ANGELS CAN BE BOTH GOOD AND EVIL

As we've seen, angels have moral agency. They can be held morally accountable for their actions. And it seems there was a point in time when some angels chose to rebel against God, led by the devil or Satan (Jude 6). Satan, says Graham Cole, 'is an active agent, with powers of intelligence, intentionality, and communication.'[5] The Bible warns us: 'Be alert and of sober mind. Your enemy the devil prowls around like a roaring lion looking for someone to devour' (1 Pet. 5:8).

Satan is sometimes known as 'Lucifer' and this may have originally been his name (just as Gabriel is called 'Gabriel'). It means 'light-bearer'. The word 'Lucifer' appears in older translations of the Bible, but modern translations tend to translate it 'morning star' or 'day star' (Isa. 14:12; it's the Latin name for the planet Venus). The point is it has a positive connotation. Satan was once an angel who illuminated heaven with his presence. But in his pride he sought to rise above God and as a result he was cast down (1 Tim. 3:6). Angels will be held morally accountable for their actions, and this means Satan and his angels will be judged eternally by God (Rev. 20:10).

It seems an individual angel will be either all good or all bad. Human beings are more complex and ambiguous. People are made in God's image, but now that image is warped by our sin. So we're capable of both great acts of kindness and unspeakable acts of cruelty. We can show humility, creativity,

5. Christopher J. H. Wright, *The God I Don't Understand*, (Zondervan, 2008), 37.

courage and love, and yet we can also show pride, negativity, cowardice and hatred. Only in movies are people all good (the 'goodies') while others are all bad (the 'baddies'). The fault line between good and evil runs through the middle of each one of us. I'm both good and bad; I commit acts of both generosity and evil. But with angels that fault line separates one angel from another. The good angels always perfectly obey God so that to some degree they share His holiness and are sometimes called 'holy angels' (Luke 9:26; Rev. 14:10). Meanwhile, the bad angels are consistently hell-bent on opposing God. They seem now to be incapable of any kindness or sympathy.

Could more good angels change sides in the future? There's no suggestion of this in the Bible, and most theologians think both good and bad angels are now fixed in their current state. The eighteenth-century American theologian Jonathan Edwards said, 'The angels that stood [that is, remained faithful to God] are doubtless confirmed in holiness, and their allegiance to God; so that they never will sin, and they are out of every danger of it.' Edwards argues that this fixed state was brought about as the full extent of God's displeasure at sin was revealed in the condemnation of Satan, and as the full extent of God's love was revealed in the salvation of the church.[6]

ANGELS APPEAR TO BE STRUCTURED IN HIERARCHIES

There are a couple of references in the Bible to 'archangels' (1 Thess. 4:16; Jude 9). The prefix 'arch-' means 'first' or 'primary'(either in origin or authority). So it seems an archangel is to an angel what an archbishop is to a bishop. They are

---

6. Jonathan Edwards, 'Miscellaneous Observations: Angels', *The Works of Jonathan Edwards, Volume 2*, (Ball, Arnold & Co, 1840), 604.

over-angels or angelic overseers. The archangel Michael is of sufficient standing that he can contend with the devil (Jude 9).

It may be, too that when the Bible talks about 'thrones or powers or rulers or authorities' (Col. 1:16) it is describing different types or levels of angelic being. Isaiah 6:2 speaks of 'seraphim', winged angels who serve in God's throne room. The Bible more often speaks of 'cherubim' (Gen. 3:24). In English we normally make a word plural by add the letter 's': one dog becomes many dogs. In the Hebrew language in which the Old Testament was written you can make a plural by adding 'im'. So 'seraphim' and 'cherubim' are the plural of 'seraph' and 'cherub'. God is often said to be 'enthroned between the cherubim' (2 Sam. 6:2; 2 Kings 19:15; Ps. 80:1; 99:1). This was pictured in the construction of the ark of covenant. The ark was modelled on an ancient royal footstool. The idea is that God sits enthroned in heaven, but His feet rest (symbolically) on the ark in the midst of God's people. And the ark was flanked by two golden cherubim whose wings stretch across its top (Exod. 25:18-20; 1 Sam. 4:4). Sometimes cherubim are pictured as having four faces (Ezek. 10:14); and sometimes as having two (Ezek. 41:18-19). These discrepancies suggest we are reading highly symbolic presentations rather than literal descriptions. Nor can we know whether the attributes of seraphim and cherubim apply to other angels.

Some people have come up with elaborate schemes for distinguishing different types of angels. An anonymous fifth-century monk known as Pseudo-Dionysius (because people thought he was the Dionysius mentioned in Acts 17:34) wrote a book called *The Celestial Hierarchy* which was very popular in the medieval church. Pseudo-Dionysius outlined an elaborate hierarchy of angels organised in three ranks each consisting of three types of angel:

1. seraphim, cherubim and thrones
2. dominations, powers and authorities
3. principalities, archangels and angels

This was important for Pseudo-Dionysius because he also developed a corresponding hierarchical pattern in his book *The Ecclesiastical Hierarchy* of sacraments and church offices which help the faithful progress towards communion with God.

But there is very little biblical basis for these assertions. We cannot know for sure whether 'thrones or powers or rulers or authorities' are generic terms or refer to different grades of angel, and we certainly cannot know how any hierarchy of angels might be organised.

ANGELS ARE NOT ALL-POWERFUL

We've seen what the Bible positively affirms about angels. But there are some important things that are never said of angels in the Bible. Angels are powerful, but they are not all-powerful. Their knowledge is limited. They do not know the future (unless God tells it to them so they can pass on this knowledge to people). The Apostle Peter says that when the prophets of the Old Testament spoke of God's coming salvation Jesus, they didn't have the full picture of how what they predicted would be fulfilled. Then he adds, 'Even angels long to look into these things' (1 Pet. 1:12). Even angels didn't grasp the full picture ahead of time.

Angels can move from place to place, but they cannot be in two places at once in the way that God is present everywhere. When Satan comes before God in the book of Job, we read,

'The LORD said to Satan, "Where have you come from?" Satan answered the LORD, "From roaming throughout the earth, going to and fro on it"' (Job 1:7). So, although they are spirits and therefore not constrained by physical objects (like walls), they are finite. Their location is circumscribed in some way (just as our souls are not present in multiple locations). Angels, even demons, can only operate under God's authority. Satan needs God's permission before he tests people (Job 1:11-12).

ANGELS ARE NOT MADE IN GOD'S IMAGE

In the Bible's account of creation we read:

> Then God said, 'Let us make mankind in our image, in our likeness, so that they may rule over the fish in the sea and the birds in the sky, over the livestock and all the wild animals, and over all the creatures that move along the ground.'
>
> So God created mankind in his own image,
> in the image of God he created them;
> male and female he created them (Gen. 1:26-27).

Though there are massive differences between God and us, there are some important ways in which we are similar. One of those appears to be the capacity for loving relationships. God says, 'Let us make mankind in our image' not 'Let me'. It's an early indication that God is a trinity of three persons sharing one being, living in a community of love. And God has made human beings to be a community in which there is both unity and diversity. One sign of that is that we are made male and female ('male and female he created them'). That's not because God is gendered (God is neither male nor female), but because God is diversity in unity. The angels are not gendered (like

God), but that lack of differentiation perhaps means they are less suited to reflect the diversity in unity of the Holy Trinity.

Being made in God's image is not only a characteristic, but also a role or task which humanity has been given. God makes human beings in His image 'so that they may rule over the fish … birds … animals …' (Gen. 1:26). God made human beings to be His representatives on earth and to rule under His rule. This doesn't mean He's given us the right to exploit the rest of creation; quite the opposite. He entrusted the world into our care – a privilege not given to the angels. This fact never ceased to amaze King David. In Psalm 8 he says:

> When I consider your heavens,
>   the work of your fingers,
> the moon and the stars,
>   which you have set in place,
> what is mankind that you are mindful of them,
>   human beings that you care for them?
> You have made them a little lower than the angels
>   and crowned them with glory and honour.
> You made them rulers over the works of your hands;
>   you put everything under their feet. (Ps. 8:3-6)

Human beings are lower than angels in our capacities. Nevertheless, God has crowned us with the honour of ruling over this world.

Sadly, by rejecting God's rule, human beings have made a mess of our rule of the earth. When we have authority we too often use it to exploit the earth. And the earth has been cursed by our rebellion so that it often eludes our authority. The writer of Hebrews quotes Psalm 8 and adds: 'In putting everything under them, God left nothing that is not subject to them. Yet at present we do not see everything subject to them.' The present reality doesn't match God's original intention. But then the writer adds: 'But we do see Jesus.' We don't see human rule working well; but we do see Jesus – the One in whom human rule is being restored. The writer goes on: 'But we do see Jesus, who was made lower than the angels for a little while, now crowned with glory and honour because he suffered death, so that by the grace of God he might taste death for everyone' (Heb. 2:8-9).

ANGELS ARE NOT THE OBJECTS OF GOD'S SAVING MERCY

This leads us to another thing that is not said of angels. The Son of God did not become an angel to redeem the fallen angels. Instead, He became incarnate as a human being to redeem human beings. He took on human flesh, not angelic spirit. The writer of Hebrews says:

> Since the children have flesh and blood, he too shared in their humanity so that by his death he might break the power of him who holds the power of death—that is, the devil—and free those who all their lives were held in slavery by their fear of death. For surely it is not angels he helps, but Abraham's descendants (Heb. 2:14-16).

It was the flesh and blood of human beings that Jesus shared, becoming 'fully human in every way' (Heb. 2:17). He didn't come to save angels. 'God did not spare angels when they sinned, but sent them to hell, putting them in chains of darkness to be held for judgment' (2 Pet. 2:4). Instead, Jesus came to save human beings who share the faith of Abraham.

Could God have chosen to save some or all of the fallen angels? Could Jesus have paid the price of their rebellion and sent His Spirit to open their eyes to His love? We cannot know. What we do know is that He didn't. He came instead for lost human beings. He broke the power of death over us. Death is the ultimate punishment for sin. But Jesus bore that punishment in our place so that death has no enduring claim on us.

WHO IS THE ANGEL OF THE LORD?

There's one special angel we need to consider. The Bible speaks of 'the angel of the LORD'[7] or 'the angel of God'[8] (and in one instance 'the angel of his presence'[9]). Every angel is 'of the LORD' in the sense that all angels are God's servants and are sent from Him. But this angel appears to be in a special category.

The first time we meet the angel of the LORD is in the story of Hagar. The patriarch Abraham and his wife, Sarah, appeared to be unable to have children, even though God had promised they would become a great nation. Eventually, their patience ran out and Sarah suggested Abraham sleep with her maidservant, Hagar. Hagar became pregnant, but predictably it soon turned sour as Hagar despised her mistress and Sarah began to mistreat her. So Hagar ran away into the desert. 'The angel of the LORD found Hagar near a spring in the desert' (Gen. 16:7). The angel told Hagar to return to her mistress and promised her a great future. Then we read: 'She gave this name to the LORD who spoke to her: "You are the God who

---

7. Genesis 16:7-14; 22:11, 15; Exodus 3:2; 14:19; Numbers 22:21-35; Judges 2:1-5; 5:23; 6:11-24; 13:3-21; 1 Kings 19:7; 2 Kings 1:3, 15; 19:35; 1 Chronicles 21:1-30; Psalm 34:7; 35:5-6; Isaiah 37:36; Zechariah 1:11-12; 3:1-6; 12:8; Matthew 1:20, 24.

8. Genesis 21:17; 31:11; Exodus 14:19; Judges 6:20; 13:6, 9.

9. Isaiah 63:9.

sees me," for she said, "I have now seen the One who sees me"' (Gen. 16:13). The writer says 'the angel of the Lord' spoke with her and then he says 'the Lord' spoke to her. And Hagar names the angel 'the God who sees me'. So here it appears the angel of the Lord is God Himself appearing in angelic form.

We find a similar pattern when God calls a man called Gideon to liberate the Israelites from the oppression of the Midianites (Judg. 6:11-24). The story begins with 'the angel of the Lord' coming to Gideon, but this same being is variously called 'the angel of the Lord', 'the angel of God' and 'the Lord'. 'Alas, Sovereign Lord!' said Gideon, 'I have seen the angel of the Lord face to face!' (Judg. 6:22). Moses had once asked to see God's glory and God had replied, 'You cannot see my face, for no one may see me and live' (Exod. 33:20). This is probably behind Gideon's concern about seeing the angel of the Lord 'face to face'. It suggests he thinks of the angel as God Himself.

These two stories suggest the angel of the Lord is the Lord. But it is not so straightforward.

In Gideon's story we're told 'the angel of the Lord disappeared' (Judg. 6:21). It is this vanishing act that made Gideon realise it was the angel of the Lord and exclaim, 'Alas, Sovereign Lord! I have seen the angel of the Lord face to face!' Here he talks to God about the angel as if the angel is another being. Moreover, God responds to him: 'The Lord said to him, "Peace! Do not be afraid. You are not going to die"' (Judg. 6:23). The angel of the Lord has 'disappeared', but the Lord Himself is still speaking to Gideon.

King David once ordered a census which incurred God's judgment (1 Chron. 21). We're not told precisely why God was displeased, but it was probably because it was an indication of David's self-reliance. God gives David a choice of punishment and David chooses the option of three days of plague at the hand of the angel of the LORD.

> So the LORD sent a plague on Israel, and seventy thousand men of Israel fell dead. And God sent an angel to destroy Jerusalem. But as the angel was doing so, the LORD saw it and relented concerning the disaster and said to the angel who was destroying the people, 'Enough! Withdraw your hand.' The angel of the LORD was then standing at the threshing floor of Araunah the Jebusite (1 Chron. 21:14-15).

It's clear that the LORD sent the plague and the angel of the LORD enacts that command. But here they are two different entities because the LORD spoke to the angel, telling it to relent. As a result, the judgment was paused. But the angel remained poised. So the angel of the LORD told David to build an altar and offer a sacrifice. Only then does the LORD tell the angel to put his sword back into its sheath (1 Chron. 21:27). Again the LORD is addressing the angel as someone who is not Himself. And, just in case you think this might be a different angel, a few verses later we're told David was afraid of 'the sword of the angel of the LORD' (1 Chron. 21:30). So here the angel of the LORD is someone other than God to whom God speaks.

We find a similar pattern in a vision of the prophet Zechariah. Zechariah saw horses sent out into the world to scout out information. They find the world at peace, but it's a false peace, a form of complacency. 'Then the angel of the LORD said, "LORD Almighty, how long will you withhold mercy from Jerusalem and from the towns of Judah, which you have been angry with these seventy years?" So the LORD spoke kind and comforting words to the angel who talked with me.'"

41

(Zech. 1:12-13) This time the angel of the LORD speaks to the LORD, and the LORD responds with words of comfort.

So sometimes the angel of the LORD appears to be the LORD Himself, and sometimes the angel of the LORD appears to be someone other than the LORD. At this point you might be wondering whether the angel of the LORD is the Son of God, appearing temporally before His incarnation. This would explain why he's sometimes identified with the LORD (since the Son is God) and sometimes differentiated from the LORD (since the Father, Son and Spirit are three persons). This interpretation was common among the church fathers,[10] though not universal.[11]

But, while it is possible the angel of the LORD is Jesus, there are problems with this view. For one thing the angel of the Lord appears in the stories of the birth of Jesus:

> An angel of the Lord appeared to him in a dream and said, 'Joseph son of David, do not be afraid to take Mary home as your wife, because what is conceived in her is from the Holy Spirit. She will give birth to a son, and you are to give him the name Jesus' (Matt. 1:20-21).

Here the angel of the Lord talks to Joseph about Jesus and refers to Jesus as another person. The angel stands before Joseph (albeit in a dream) while Jesus is already growing in the womb of Mary. It's possible that Matthew uses the phrase simply to describe an angel from God without intending to evoke the Old

---

10. For a defence of this position see Douglas F. Kelly, *Systematic Theology: Volume One,* (Christian Focus, 2008), 479-483.

11. See Augustine in *On the Trinity*, Book 3, Chapter 11 in *The Nicene and Post-Nicene Fathers: First Series* Volume 3, ed. Philip Schaff, (Hendrickson, 1994), 65-68.

Testament 'angel of the LORD'. But this is unlikely: Matthew was a Jew who wrote for Jewish readers and packed his account of Jesus with Old Testament allusions. The fingerprints of the Old Testament are all over Matthew's account of the birth of Jesus. It's much more probable that Matthew intentionally wants to convey the idea that the great angel of the LORD has come once more, this time to announce the imminent arrival of the LORD Himself: 'Immanuel', 'God with us' (Matt. 1:23).

One of the appearances of the angel of the LORD was when Moses met God at the burning bush: 'There the angel of the LORD appeared to him in flames of fire from within a bush' (Exod. 3:2). We're told that God called to Moses from the bush (Exod. 3:4), but the individual he saw was 'the angel of the LORD'. In a speech before the Jewish Council the first Christian martyr Stephen interprets 'the angel of the LORD' in this story as the appearance of an angel (Acts 7:30). Stephen comments: '[Moses] was sent to be their ruler and deliverer by God himself, through the angel who appeared to him in the bush' (Acts 7:35). Notice that God does the sending, but He does so through the angel. The angel, here, is not identified with God, but he is identified as one through whom God acts (in this case to call Moses to be the liberator of God's people).

St Augustine argued that, since the essence of God is invisible, when God appeared in bodily form to people in the Old Testament He did so through angels. For example, at a key moment in the life of Jacob, one of the founding fathers of the nation of Israel, he meets a man in the night with whom he wrestles. It's a full-blooded physical struggle which leaves Jacob with a lifelong limp. Yet, as the story unfolds it becomes clear that his combatant is God Himself. Although there is no mention of an angel in the original account in the book of Genesis (Gen. 32:22-32), the prophet Hosea identifies the stranger in the night as an angel (Hos. 12:4). So it seems God appears to Jacob through an angel as a man. 'Those words and bodily appearances,' says Augustine, 'which were given to these ancient fathers of ours before the incarnation of the Saviour, when God was said to appear, were wrought by angels: whether themselves speaking or doing something in the person of God.'[12] The Bible speaks of this as the LORD appearing (rather than describing it as an angelic appearance) just as we might say, 'The judge said the accused was guilty' even if that announcement was actually made by the court clerk.[13] Augustine's concern (in addition to following 'the divine declarations from the Holy Scriptures') is to preserve the uniqueness of the incarnation: only in Christ is God made flesh.

So it's probably best to see the angel of the LORD as God's personal representative rather than a direct appearance of Christ. But it may not be an either/or choice. The Son is the eternal Word of God, the One in whom God reveals Himself. Every revelation of God is made through the Son – the Son is, as it were, God's faculty of communication. So when we say God appeared in bodily form through an angel it might be more accurate to say God revealed Himself in the Son appearing through an angel (Rev. 1:1-2). The angel of the LORD is not the Son, but makes the Son present in or through the angel to communicate God's message.

---

12. Augustine, *On The Trinity*, 3.11.27, in *The Nicene and Post-Nicene Fathers: First Series* Volume 3, ed. Philip Schaff, (Hendrickson, 1994), 67-68.

13. Augustine, 'On The Trinity', 3.11.22-23, in *The Nicene and Post-Nicene Fathers: First Series* Volume 3, ed. Philip Schaff, (Hendrickson, 1994), 65.

Because the angel of the LORD is God's representative, the words he speaks are the words of God and the acts he performs are the acts of God. This is why he can be identified as God. He is, as it were, an extension of God's presence and activity. But he is not God Himself and this is why we read of him being spoken to by God and speaking to God. Nevertheless, God appears and interacts with people through the agency of the angel of the LORD so that people have a real encounter with God.

3.

Where are Angels?

Just as angels don't have physical bodies, so they don't live in our physical world. Instead, they live in heaven. But what and where is heaven?

In popular thought 'heaven' is the place where God lives and where good people go when they die. But the Bible's portrait of heaven is a bit more nuanced than this. Sometimes the Bible uses the word 'heavens' to speak of the physical universe beyond the earth – what today we call 'outer space'. And sometimes the Bible uses 'heaven' as a picture of God's reign. While Mark and Luke speak of God's reign as 'the kingdom of God', Matthew uses the term 'the kingdom of heaven'. Matthew is probably following the Jewish convention of substituting God's name with other words to avoid any misuse of that name. But it is striking that 'heaven' substitutes for 'God' in this description of God's reign. God reigns on earth in the sense that nothing happens outside His control. But people don't freely submit to His law. So on earth His rule is rejected. We know this from our own experience. Turn on the television or scroll through any social media feed and people are not obviously trying to live in obedience to God. But the angels in heaven obey God's rule perfectly. Hence in the Lord's Prayer Jesus teaches to pray: 'Your kingdom come, your will be done, on earth as it is in heaven' (Matt. 6:10).

IN ANOTHER DIMENSION

But there's another sense in which the Bible speaks of heaven. When the Apostle Paul writes to the church in Ephesus he uses the phrase 'the heavenly realms' a number of times (Eph. 1:3, 20; 2:6; 3:10; 6:12). 'The heavenly realms' describes another realm separate from our physical world. The Bible speaks of 'heaven' as 'above'. Jesus, for example, 'ascends' into heaven. But this is a symbol of transcendence rather than a literal location in space. We mustn't think of heaven as somewhere beyond the edge of the universe. It is not as if, were we to travel to the edge of space and then go a bit further, we would eventually reach it. It is better to think of the heavenly realms as another dimension within creation – a dimension alongside physical height, length and breadth. It's a dimension beyond our natural senses – it's not a place we can see or hear. But it is part of creation.

This might sound a bit weird and that's because it is weird! It's beyond anything within our experience. But the universe is a weird place! Consider dark matter. Physicists think dark matter makes up around 85 per cent of the universe. Without it galaxies could not have formed and without it they would fly apart. It is, as it were, the gravitational ballast that holds galaxies together. Yet dark matter is theoretical. No one has seen or experienced it. It must exist, but it remains undetected, perhaps undetectable. Maybe there is some link between dark matter and the heavenly realms. At the very least dark matter reminds us that the structure of the universe remains mysterious. There are levels and layers we cannot comprehend. Just because something cannot be detected doesn't mean it does not exist.

The heavenly realms are also a contested realm because not all angels are good. So, while 'heaven' (singular) is used to represent the scope of God's rule, 'the heavenly realms' are more complex. In Ephesians 6:12 Paul says: 'For our struggle is not against flesh and blood, but against the rulers, against the authorities, against the powers of this dark world and against the spiritual forces of evil in the heavenly realms.' The heavenly realms are populated not just by the spiritual forces of good (angels), but also by 'the spiritual forces of evil' (demons). So now there's a battle going on between angels and demons. The good news, as we'll see, is that Christ has conquered through His death and resurrection. So God has 'seated him at his right hand in the heavenly realms, far above all rule and authority, power and dominion' (Eph. 1:20-21). The struggle continues, but the decisive victory has been won.

WHEN HEAVEN TOUCHES EARTH

Though the heavenly realms, along with the beings that inhabit them, are normally beyond our senses, they do sometimes interact with our world. The patriarch Jacob was given a graphic picture of this in a dream: 'He saw a stairway resting on the earth, with its top reaching to heaven, and the angels of God were ascending and descending on it' (Gen. 28:12). Angels can appear to human beings and perform tasks in our world.

This also means the battle between the forces of good and evil spills out of heaven onto earth. Christians can be caught up in this battle. So Paul has to say, 'Put on the full armour of God, so that you can take your stand against the devil's schemes' (Eph. 6:11).

While they do not have bodies, angels can take on bodily form. When angels do appear they seem to be either glorious to the point of being frightening or to go undetected. Hebrews 13:2 says: 'Do not forget to show hospitality to strangers, for by so doing some people have shown hospitality to angels without knowing it.' It's probably an allusion to an occasion when the patriarch Abraham welcomed three travellers (Gen. 18:1-15; see also Gen. 19:1-14; Judg. 6:11-18; 13:3-22). They initially appear to be three human beings, but as the story unfolds it becomes clear that they are the LORD and two angels in human form.

THE HEAVENLY COURT

The heavenly realms are sometimes portrayed as a royal council ...

> The heavens praise your wonders, LORD,
> your faithfulness too, in the assembly of the holy ones.
> For who in the skies above can compare with the LORD?
> Who is like the LORD among the heavenly beings?
> In the council of the holy ones God is greatly feared;
> he is more awesome than all who surround him (Ps. 89:5-7).[1]

Or a judicial courtroom ...

---

1. Psalm 82 may also describe the heavenly council though D. A. Carson argues it refers to the assembly of Israel. See D. A. Carson, *The Gospel According to John*, (IVP, 1991), 397-399 and Michael Wilcock, *Psalms 73-150*, (IVP, 2001), 40-43.

As I looked,

thrones were set in place,

    and the Ancient of Days took his seat …

Thousands upon thousands attended him;

    ten thousand times ten thousand stood before him.

The court was seated,

    and the books were opened (Dan. 7:9-10).

Heaven is God's throne room and the spirits are His courtiers. Jonathan Edwards describes angels as 'the nobles and barons of the court of heaven … dignified servants in the palace of the King of Kings.'[2]

The story of Job began in the heavenly council. 'One day the angels came to present themselves before the LORD,' says Job 1:6, 'and Satan also came with them.' Job was singled out by God as a model of righteous living. But Satan suggested Job only worships God because God had blessed him. So God allowed Satan to remove Job's blessings and so the story began. But this conversation took place in the royal court of heaven. The angels came, says Old Testament scholar David Clines, 'as courtiers before their king in order to make their reports and receive instructions.'[3]

On another occasion King Ahab, the king of the ten northern tribes of Israel, wanted the help of King Jehoshaphat, the king of the two southern tribes. Ahab proposed an alliance to recapture the town of Ramoth Gilead. Jehoshaphat was open to the idea, but suggested they first ought to consult the

---

2. Jonathan Edwards, 'Miscellaneous Observations: Angels', *The Works of Jonathan Edwards, Volume 2,* (Ball, Arnold & Co, 1840), 607.

3. David Clines, *Job 1-20*, Word Biblical Commentary Volume 19, (Word Books, 1989), 19.

Lord. So, 400 tame in-house prophets were summoned, all of whom predicted success. But King Jehoshaphat could see they were yes-men, primed to say whatever King Ahab wanted to hear. So he said, 'Is there no longer a prophet of the Lord here whom we can inquire of?' Ahab replied: 'There is still one prophet through whom we can inquire of the Lord, but I hate him because he never prophesies anything good about me, but always bad. He is Micaiah son of Imlah' (1 Kings 22:7-8). It's a revealing statement. Ahab was not interested in hearing from God. He only wanted to hear what he wanted to hear. The messenger who summoned Micaiah urged him to agree with the other prophets. But that's not how God's Word works! 'As surely as the Lord lives,' replied Micaiah, 'I can tell him only what the Lord tells me' (1 Kings 22:14). Ahab was like people today who reject aspects of the Bible's teaching because they find them unsettling or out of set with our culture. Micaiah highlighted how crazy this is by playing along and promising success: 'Attack and be victorious ... for the Lord will give it into the king's hand' (1 Kings 22:15). You can hear his world-weary tone even in the written account! Everyone could detect the irony. Even King Ahab demanded to hear the real truth. And so Micaiah duly declared that the campaign will end in disaster. At this point Micaiah continued:

> Therefore hear the word of the Lord: I saw the Lord sitting on his throne with all the multitudes of heaven standing round him on his right and on his left. And the Lord said, 'Who will entice Ahab into attacking Ramoth Gilead and going to his death there?'
>
> One suggested this, and another that. Finally, a spirit came forward, stood before the Lord and said, 'I will entice him.'
>
> 'By what means?' the Lord asked.

'I will go out and be a deceiving spirit in the mouths of all his prophets,' he said.

'You will succeed in enticing him,' said the LORD. 'Go and do it.'

So now the LORD has put a deceiving spirit in the mouths of all these prophets of yours. The LORD has decreed disaster for you (1 Kings 22:19-23).

King Ahab thought he was plotting a military victory in his royal courtroom. But what was actually taking place was the outworking of a plan devised in the royal courtroom of heaven. God and the spirits or angels had met together. God had decided it was time to judge Ahab through military defeat and an angelic spirit had suggested how this might be accomplished through the enticement of false prophets.

When the prophet Jeremiah condemned false prophets, he did so by pointing out that they have had no access to the deliberations of the heavenly court.

This is what the LORD Almighty says:
'Do not listen to what the prophets are prophesying to you;
    they fill you with false hopes.
They speak visions from their own minds,
    not from the mouth of the LORD.

They keep saying to those who despise me,
    "The LORD says: You will have peace."
And to all who follow the stubbornness of their hearts
    they say, "No harm will come to you."
But which of them has stood in the council of the LORD
    to see or to hear his word?
Who has listened and heard his word?' (Jer. 23:16-18).

We shouldn't imagine God holds a literal court with angels literally attending some kind of council chamber. Christopher Ash says: 'Presumably this language of God's sitting surrounded by a heavenly council is anthropomorphic [using human characteristics to picture God]. God does not literally sit at the head of a council any more than he literally has hands or feet.'[4] Its purpose, Ash suggests, is powerfully to express the way the world is governed. It is not a world of competing gods, nor of good and evil locked in an uncertain battle. But neither is God's rule so absolute that there is no room for other agents. Instead God's rule is supreme and unchallenged, but angels and humans also shape events.

> The Bible portrays for us a world that lies under the absolute supremacy and sovereignty of the Creator, who has no rivals, who is unique, such that there is no god like him. And yet he does not govern the world as the sole supernatural power. He governs the world by the means of and through the agency of a multiplicity of supernatural powers, some of whom are evil.[5]

ANGELS AT LARGE IN THE WORLD

There are indications that spiritual beings may shape or energise the tyrannical rule of human empires. Daniel saw a vision of a gleaming man who said to him:

> 'Do not be afraid, Daniel. Since the first day that you set your mind to gain understanding and to humble yourself before your God, your words were heard, and I have come in response to them. But the prince of the Persian kingdom resisted me twenty-one days. Then Michael, one of the chief princes, came

---

4. Christopher Ash, *Job: The Wisdom of the Cross*, (Crossway, 2004), 40.

5. Christopher Ash, *Job: The Wisdom of the Cross*, (Crossway, 2004), 41.

to help me, because I was detained there with the king of Persia. Now I have come to explain to you what will happen to your people in the future, for the vision concerns a time yet to come' (Dan. 10:12-14).

Elsewhere 'Michael' is the name of an archangel and this is likely to be the Michael described in this passage as 'one of the chief princes'. So the word 'princes' is being used here to refer to spiritual beings. This would make 'the prince of the Persian kingdom' a spiritual being who undergirded or supported in some way the rule of 'the king of Persia'. It's worth noting, though, that in the following chapter human conflict is described without any reference to angelic influence. If human empires are shaped by angels then this is only one factor among others.

In Isaiah 14 the prophet Isaiah condemns the hubris of the king of Babylon. But the language moves beyond earthly realities to heavenly realities:

How you have fallen from heaven,
    morning star, son of the dawn!
You have been cast down to the earth,
    you who once laid low the nations!
You said in your heart,
    'I will ascend to the heavens;
I will raise my throne
    above the stars of God;
I will sit enthroned on the mount of assembly,
    on the utmost heights of Mount Zaphon.
I will ascend above the tops of the clouds;
    I will make myself like the Most High.'
But you are brought down to the realm of the dead,
    to the depths of the pit (Isa. 14:12-15).

While most modern commentators see this as a description of an end to the vaulting ambitions of Babylonian imperial power, the church fathers saw it as a description of the fall of Satan. It's not an either/or choice. The Babylonian empire was the latest manifestation of satanic power. So its fall on earth would mirror and repeat Satan's fall from heaven.

We find the same pattern in Ezekiel 28. Verses 1-10 clearly describe a human ruler while verses 11-19 appear to describe a spiritual being behind this ruler. The first is a mortal, albeit one with exalted pretensions (Ezek. 28:9) while the second is described as a 'cherub':

> You were in Eden,
>> the garden of God …
> You were anointed as a guardian cherub,
>> for so I ordained you …
> You were blameless in your ways
>> from the day you were created
>> till wickedness was found in you.
> Through your widespread trade
>> you were filled with violence,
>> and you sinned.
> So I drove you in disgrace from the mount of God,
>> and I expelled you, guardian cherub (Ezek. 28:13-16).

Again, it is likely to be a double reference both to an historical human being and to Satan who underwrote his power. The reference to 'widespread trade' suggests a human ruler while the expulsion from Eden suggests Satan. They reflect one another in their pride, and the fall of the imperial power would mirror the fall of Satan.

Some people have taken these hints and claimed that particular spirits control specific geographic regions or institutions. There may be confirmation of this idea in Deuteronomy 32:8. In the New International Version it reads: 'When the Most High gave the nations their inheritance, when he divided all mankind, he set up boundaries for the peoples according to the number of the sons of Israel.' But the Septuagint (the early Greek translation of the Old Testament) and the Dead Sea Scrolls speak of 'the number of the sons of God'. Both the Septuagint and the Dead Sea Scrolls date from about 300 years before Jesus, but after the Old Testament, though it is possible they represent an older tradition. The English Standard Version translates the verse: 'He fixed the borders of the peoples according to the number of the sons of God' while the New Living Translation goes further and paraphrases it as 'according to the number in his heavenly court'. This reading would suggest the nations were placed under the supervision of angels (here called 'sons of god') while Israel was reserved for God Himself. But it's all a bit uncertain and fragmentary. Maybe individual angels are linked with specific nations or regions. But the Bible does not state this explicitly. And a good principle to follow is that, when it comes to spiritual matters, we clearly don't need to know what the Bible doesn't tell us clearly.

Nevertheless some people have developed a case for what they call 'warfare prayer' through which, they claim, we should counter the influence of territorial spirits.[6] This goes beyond prayer to God for a region (which the Bible commends). Instead, it involves prayer directed to the spirits themselves,

---

6. See, for example, C. Peter and F. Douglas Pennoyer (eds.), *Wrestling with Dark Angels: Supernatural Forces in Spiritual Warfare*, (Monarch, 1990).

commanding them to retreat, sometimes through symbolic actions or by reclaiming an area in Jesus' name. Naming spirits and spiritual mapping are sometimes seen as an important feature of this approach.

Jesus and the apostles did address evil spirits when they exorcised them from individuals. But there is no precedent for scaling this up to address the supposed spirits of territories. The New Testament does talk about spiritual warfare, but it presents it in terms of resisting temptation, being faithful in prayer and continuing to proclaim the good news of Jesus (Eph. 6:10-20). What does spiritual warfare look like? asks David Powlison: 'It looks like the Christian life.'[7]

The fact that we are told so little about angelic hierarchies and have no explicit command to engage in so-called 'warfare prayer' suggests it does not play the central role in mission that is sometimes claimed for it. Indeed, missiologist Paul Hiebert argues 'warfare prayer' reflects a tendency towards dualism[8] – the belief that the world is an uncertain struggle between the forces of good and evil. So its advocates urge us to do battle with demonic forces to allow God to act or 'release' His power, instead of confidently praying to the sovereign God.[9]

---

7. David Powlison, 'The Classical Model', in *Understanding Spiritual Warfare: Four Views*, eds. James K. Beilby and Paul Rhodes Eddy, (Baker, 2012), 98.

8. Paul Hiebert, 'Spiritual Warfare: A Biblical Perspective', *Mission Focus*, Vol. 20, No. 3, September 1992, 41-46.

9. For more on this issue see David Powlison, *Power Encounters: Reclaiming Spiritual Warfare,* (Baker, 1995); Chuck Lowe, *Territorial Spirits and World Evangelisation?* (Mentor/OMF, 1998); and Tim Chester, *The Message of Prayer,* (IVP, 2003), 220-231.

4.

What do Angels do all day?

When I was a small child one of my favourite books was *What Do People Do All Day?* by Richard Scarry. Each page explained what a different job involved along with quirky illustrations of animals doing the roles. Many years later, when I was introduced to money supply theory in economics lessons, I can remember thinking, 'I know how this works because in *What Do People Do All Day?* Grocer Cat gave money to Farmer Alfalfa (depicted as a goat) for his corn who then spent it on a new suit from Stiches the Tailor (a mouse) who then spent it on an egg whisk'—I have no idea why an egg whisk was chosen—'so the same money was used multiple times.' My childhood copy of the book fell apart a long time ago. But recently I was delighted to be able to buy another copy in a second-hand bookshop.

In an homage to Richard Scarry, I've called this chapter: What do angels do all day? We've thought about what angels are and where they are located. But what do they do? Sadly, I can't provide quirky animal-based illustrations. But we can discover what the Bible says about the role of angels.

ANGELS HAVE A JOB TITLE

The word 'angel' means 'messenger'. So, while the word 'spirit' describes what angels are, the word 'angel' is essentially their job title – it describes what they do. Angels are messengers who pass on God's Word. Because of God's radical transcendence over human beings, His communication must be mediated and angels play a role in this mediation. They are not the mediator – that is Jesus Christ. Jesus is the Word by whom and in which God speaks. He is the God-man who links humanity and divinity in His own person. He is therefore able to 'translate', as it were, the thoughts of God into the words of humanity. All divine communication comes through Christ. Nevertheless, angels play a role in passing on that communication, especially before the incarnation of Christ.

As we've seen, Jacob dreamed of 'a stairway resting on the earth, with its top reaching to heaven, and the angels of God were ascending and descending on it' (Gen. 28:12). It's a picture of angels coming to earth with a message from God. Angels bridge heaven and earth. Jesus added an interesting twist on this vision. Speaking to someone called Nathaniel he said, 'Very truly I tell you, you will see "heaven open, and the angels of God ascending and descending on" the Son of Man' (John 1:51). Jesus echoes Jacob's vision of angels ascending and descending, but now they are ascending and descending on the Son of Man, Jesus' favourite way of referring to Himself. Angels are going to continue their role of acting in the world on

God's behalf, but they will do so on the basis of the work and authority of Jesus.

Angels appeared at key moments in the story of Jesus. It was angels who announced His birth. An angel strengthened Jesus in the Garden of Gethsemane as He contemplated His imminent death (Luke 22:43). And it was an angel who rolled away the stone covering the entrance to the tomb in which Jesus was buried (Matt. 28:2). The same angel explained to the women who had come to the tomb that Jesus had risen (Matt. 28:5-7). And what seems to be two angels appeared as Jesus passed through the clouds into heaven and they declared that Jesus would one day return in a similar fashion (Acts 1:10-11).

The most obvious way angels pass on God's Word is by conveying messages directly from God to human beings. The majority of angelic appearances recorded in the Scriptures involve an angel passing on a message from God. Sometimes they do this while someone is dreaming and sometimes they do it through a physical appearance. On at least one occasion they are sent to interpret a dream (Dan. 8:15-27). While the Apostle Paul was being brought as a prisoner to Rome, the ship in which he was being transported ran into a storm. Eventually the crew gave up hope. But Paul declared: 'Last night an angel of the God to whom I belong and whom I serve stood beside me and said, "Do not be afraid, Paul. You must stand trial before Caesar; and God has graciously given you the lives of all who sail with you"' (Acts 27:23-24).

Indeed, angels hardly ever share their own thoughts, and when they do it is because human beings have questioned the message they have brought from God. When Zechariah questioned the message brought to him by the angel Gabriel, Gabriel responded: 'I am Gabriel. I stand in the presence of God, and I have been sent to speak to you and to tell you this good news' (Luke 1:19). These appear to be Gabriel's own thoughts rather than an integral part of God's original message. Even then, it is striking that their intent was to reinforce the divine message Gabriel had been sent by God to deliver.

The Bible also suggests that angels had a role in the delivery of the Law of Moses. Moses says God came to Mount Sinai with 'myriads of holy ones' (Deut. 33:2). Stephen talks about 'the angel who spoke to [Moses] on Mount Sinai' (Acts 7:38). 'The law was given through angels,' says Galatians 3:19, 'and entrusted to a mediator.' In this case the mediator was Moses, but Moses is a picture of Jesus, the ultimate mediator between God and humanity. The precise role played by angels in passing on the law is unclear.

ANGELS ARE OUR BODYGUARDS

'Are not all angels ministering spirits sent to serve those who will inherit salvation?' says Hebrews 1:14. Angels care for God's people. 'The angel of the LORD encamps around those who fear him, and he delivers them,' says Psalm 34:7. At one point the archangel Michael is described as 'the great prince who protects your people' (Dan. 12:1). And Psalm 91:11-12 says:

> For [the LORD] will command his angels concerning you
>   to guard you in all your ways;
> they will lift you up in their hands,
>   so that you will not strike your foot against a stone.

We see numerous examples of angels caring for God's people throughout the Bible story. After God had delivered His people from slavery in Egypt, He said, 'See, I am sending an angel ahead of you to guard you along the way and to bring you to the place I have prepared' (Exod. 23:20). In the following verse He added, 'my name is with him' (ESV). In other words, the angel carries God's executive authority. A police officer is not acting on his own authority when he says, 'Open up in the name of the law.' He is acting on behalf of the state. In the same way, angels do not act by their own authority, but on God's behalf or in His name.

Angels provide for God's people. At one point the prophet Elijah fled in terror from the wrath of Queen Jezebel. He journeyed for a day into the desert, eventually collapsing under a bush and praying to die. 'I have had enough, LORD,' he said. 'Take my life' (1 Kings 19:4). Then he slept. 'All at once an angel touched him and said, "Get up and eat." He looked around, and there by his head was some bread baked over hot coals, and a jar of water. He ate and drank and then lay down again' (1 Kings 19:5-6). Did the angel do the baking? We're not told. But the angel ensured Elijah had food – not once, but twice (1 Kings 5:7-8). Elijah was strengthened for a forty-day journey to a meeting with God through which the prophet regained his composure and purpose.

Angels protect God's people. Several hundred years before the coming of Jesus, the Persian Emperor Darius was persuaded to pass a law forbidding his subjects to call on anyone—whether a god or human being—other than Darius himself. The primary aim of those behind this scheme was to entrap a faithful Jew called Daniel. They knew Daniel would continue praying to the true God, the God of Israel. And they were right: Daniel was caught in the act. Darius, who had a high regard for Daniel, could not make an exception to a law he himself had passed. So Daniel was famously thrown into a den of lions. The following day King Darius went to the den and called out, 'Daniel, servant of the living God, has your God, whom you serve continually, been able to rescue you from the lions?' Presumably, Darius said this more in hope than expectation. But Daniel answered, 'May the king live forever! My God sent his angel, and he shut the mouths of the lions. They have not hurt me, because I was found innocent in his sight' (Dan. 6:20-22). God rescued Daniel through the intervention of an angel.

Angels guide God's people. Angels not only rescue God's people, they also provide direction. When Abraham wanted to find a wife for his son among his own people, he commissioned a servant to go back to his homeland in search of a suitable bride with the words:

> The LORD, the God of heaven, who brought me out of my father's household and my native land and who spoke to me and promised me on oath, saying, 'To your offspring I will give this land' – he will send his angel before you so that you can get a wife for my son from there (Gen. 24:7).

In the New Testament, too, we see angels providing guidance. Philip met a royal official alongside a desert road, told him about Jesus and as a result the Christian message travelled to Ethiopia. But it was an angel who directed Philip to what would otherwise appear to have been a chance rendezvous (Acts 8:26).

Even the incarnate Jesus received support from angels. Though He remained fully divine, at His incarnation He became truly human with all the physical and bodily limitations that entails. So after His forty-day fast and His tempting by the devil, we read: 'Then the devil left him, and angels came and attended him' (Matt. 4:11). We mustn't think of Jesus as a kind of superhuman. Hebrews 2:17 says He is like us, 'fully human in every way'. He 'has been tempted in every way, just as we are – yet he did not sin' (Heb. 4:15). So the forty-day fast would have left Him weak and the intensity of the encounter with Satan would have exhausted Him. In this state He needed help from angels. The same is true at the other end of His ministry. On the night before His crucifixion, as He prayed in the Garden of Gethsemane, we're told 'his sweat was like drops of blood falling to the ground' (Luke 22:44). He wrestled with the prospect of the cross: both shrinking from its horror and committed to the salvation of His people that it would achieve. In this anguish, we read, 'an angel from heaven appeared to him and strengthened him' (Luke 22:43).

As we've noted, Hebrews 13:2 says: 'Do not forget to show hospitality to strangers, for by so doing some people have shown hospitality to angels without knowing it.' It seems it is possible for human beings to serve angels without realising we are doing so. It is clearly intended as an exhortation to show love to strangers. But it also reminds us that angels may act in our lives without us realising. The kindness of strangers may actually be the provision of angels. 'When a car suddenly swerves from hitting us, when we suddenly find footing to keep from being swept along in a raging river, when we walk unscathed in a dangerous neighbourhood, should we not suspect that God has sent his angels to protect us? ... It seems right that we should do so.'[1] I suspect we have encountered angels more often than we will ever realise.

---

1. Wayne Grudem, *Systematic Theology*, (IVP, 1994), 406.

GUARDIAN ANGELS OR GUARDED BY ANGELS?

When it comes to angels, a common feature of popular thinking is the belief in guardian angels. Some people believe everyone has a guardian angel, while others believe children have a specific angel designated to care for them. The church father Jerome said, 'The dignity of a human soul is great, for each has an angel appointed to guard it.'[2] The Eastern Orthodox church believes God assigns an angel to guard Christians at their baptism.

The idea of guardian angels is derived from the words of Jesus in Matthew 18:10: 'See that you do not despise one of these little ones. For I tell you that their angels in heaven always see the face of my Father in heaven.'

The first question to address is, Who are 'these little ones' who receive angelic protection? The answer comes immediately before this statement when Jesus says we have to become 'like little children' to enter God's kingdom (Matt. 18:3). So 'these little ones' are those who renounce self-reliance and entrust themselves like children to Jesus. It's a way of describing true Christians. In verse 6 Jesus condemns anyone who harms 'these little ones', that is, His people. Elsewhere He makes the link between 'these little ones' and His followers explicit: 'And if anyone gives even a cup of cold water to one of these little ones who is my disciple,' He says in Matthew 10:42, 'Truly I tell you, that person will certainly not lose their reward.' Who are these little ones? The disciples of Jesus. So the promise of angelic protection in Matthew 18:10 is not made to people in general, nor to children. It is made to Christians, to those who have come like children and put their faith in Jesus.

---

2. Cited in Graham A. Cole, *Against the Darkness*, (Crossway, 2019), 71.

Does each Christian, then, have a specific guardian angel? This is not quite what Jesus says. 'Their angels' certainly suggests angels have a role in protecting God's people. This is what we find elsewhere in the Bible, as we've seen. But the plural ('their angels') means it's unlikely we each have one specific angel assigned to protect us. John Calvin says, 'We ought to hold as a fact that the care of each one of us is not the task of one angel only, but all with one consent watch over our salvation.'[3] One angel might be sent by God to rescue a believer (as was the case for Peter in prison in Acts 12), but that's not the same as having one angel permanently assigned to each believer. Perhaps this is the case, but we're not told this. The purpose of the passage is to emphasise the importance of God's children to Him, not to describe the exact mechanism He uses to protect them.[4] If anything, the emphasis of the Bible is even stronger than the notion of a single guardian angel. As pastor John Piper put its: 'everything angels do, everywhere in the world, at all times, is for the good of Christians'.[5] 'This subject needs no hot debate,' says the seventeenth-century Puritan Thomas Watson. 'It may suffice us to know the whole hierarchy of angels is employed

---

3. John Calvin, *The Institutes of Christian Religion,* Volume 1, trans. F.L. Battles, (Westminster Press/SCM, 1961), 1.14.7, 167.

4. B. B. Warfield proposes an alternative interpretation. He claims the 'angels' of Matthew 18:10 are the disembodied spirits of Christians after their death. They should be honoured while on earth because of the honour they will eventually receive in heaven when they will see God's face. See B. B. Warfield, 'The Angels of Christ's Little Ones', in *Selected Shorter Writings*, Volume 1, (P&R, 1970), 253-266.

5. John Piper, 'The Surprising Role of Guardian Angels', Desiring God, April 4, 2017, https://www.desiringgod.org/articles/the-surprising-role-of-guardian-angels. Accessed 6 April, 2021.

for the good of the saints … The highest angels take care of the lowest saints.'[6]

But even this is not the primary point Jesus is making in Matthew 18. His point is not that angels care for me – though that is a clear implication of what He says. Instead His main message is this: 'See that you do not despise one of these little ones' (Matt. 18:10). His point is that we should respect other Christians because angels care for them. Every Christian is like a prince or princess arriving with a heavenly entourage. You had better treat Christians with respect because they have angels on hand to protect them! Moreover, these angelic bodyguards have direct access to the Creator God for 'their angels in heaven always see the face of my Father in heaven' (Matt. 18:10). They are ready at His word to intervene to provide for, protect and guide His adopted children.

Why does God use angels when He Himself could intervene directly? It's not because God needs assistance, says John Calvin. 'He makes uses of angels to comfort our weakness.' It ought to be enough for us to know God is our protector. But God sees our fear and so 'out of his immeasurable kindness and gentleness' 'he not only promises to take care of us, but tells us he has innumerable guardians whom he has bidden to look after our safety'.[7]

ANGELS ARE GOD'S POLICE FORCE

Collectively angels are sometimes described as the 'heavenly hosts' (Ps. 148:2). It's a military term. Angels are the army

---

6. Thomas Watson, A Divine Cordial (1663), republished as *All Things for Good*, (Banner of Truth, 1986), 21.

7. John Calvin, *The Institutes of Christian Religion*, Volume 1, trans. F.L. Battles, (Westminster Press/SCM, 1961), 1.14.11, 171.

of heaven. They are God's enforcers. Angels execute God's judgment. When God wanted to prevent humanity returning to the Garden of Eden He placed angels at its entrance: 'After he drove the man out, he placed on the east side of the Garden of Eden cherubim and a flaming sword flashing back and forth to guard the way to the tree of life' (Gen. 3:24). Or when David sinned by commissioning a census, it was an angel who brought plague on the people in an act of judgment (2 Sam. 24:15-17).

King Nebuchadnezzar, the creator of the Babylonian empire, had a dream in which he saw a mighty tree being felled. The tree represented a human being who was destined to live like an animal. The fate of the tree-person was announced by an angel whom Nebuchadnezzar called 'a watcher' (Dan. 4:13, 17, 23 ESV). The prophet Daniel interpreted the dream, telling Nebuchadnezzar that he was the tree and for a period he would be humbled. And so it was: Nebuchadnezzar had some kind of breakdown and for seven years lived like a beast in the fields. In the dream the 'watcher' declared: 'The sentence is by the decree of the watchers, the decision by the word of the holy ones, to the end that the living may know that the Most High rules the kingdom of men and gives it to whom he will and sets over it the lowliest of men.' (Dan. 4:17 ESV) Angels, it seems, gather evidence of wrong-doing and carry out God's judgment – like a divine police force (Zech. 1:10-11).

Angels also appear to be involved in the final judgment. Jesus Himself said: 'If anyone is ashamed of me and my words in this adulterous and sinful generation, the Son of Man will be ashamed of them when he comes in his Father's glory with the holy angels' (Mark 8:38; see also Matt. 25:31; 2. Thess. 1:7; Jude 14-15). The Apostle Paul tells us that the return of Christ will be announced by the archangel: 'For the Lord himself will come down from heaven, with a loud command, with the voice of the archangel and with the trumpet call of God, and the dead in Christ will rise first' (1 Thess. 4:16). Elsewhere Jesus says:

> The Son of Man will send out his angels, and they will weed out of his kingdom everything that causes sin and all who do evil. They will throw them into the blazing furnace, where there will be weeping and gnashing of teeth. Then the righteous will shine like the sun in the kingdom of their Father. Whoever has ears, let them hear (Matt. 13:41-43; see also Matt. 13:49-50; 24:31).

Maxwell Davidson says angels 'function as a kind of heavenly police force, arresting offenders, presenting evidence and executing punishment.'[8]

In the last book of the Bible, the book of Revelation, the Apostle John sees a vision of four angels 'standing at the four corners of the earth, holding back the four winds of the earth' (Rev. 7:1). They are described as 'the four angels who had been given power to harm the land and the sea' (Rev. 7:2). It is a symbolic picture of the final judgment: the coming day when God will bring history to an end and judge humanity. It seems angels will enact this judgment. Already they are poised. In John's vision another angel calls out: 'Do not harm the land or the sea or the trees until we put a seal on the foreheads of the servants of our God' (Rev. 7:3). The seal on the forehead is a symbol of being marked out as belonging to God by our personal faith in Christ. The final judgment is on temporary hold. It will only take place once all God's people have responded with faith

---

8. Maxwell J. Davidson, 'Angels', in *Dictionary of Jesus and the Gospels,* eds. Joel B. Green, Jeannine K. Brown & Nicholas Perrin, 2nd. ed., (IVP, 2013), 8.

to the Christian message. The vision is a dramatic picture of the urgent need to become a Christian before it is too late.

There is also some evidence to suggest that angels were involved in the expulsion of Satan from the heavenly realms after Jesus had broken his power over humanity through the cross. Revelation 12:7-9 says:

> Then war broke out in heaven. Michael and his angels fought against the dragon, and the dragon and his angels fought back. But he was not strong enough, and they lost their place in heaven. The great dragon was hurled down – that ancient serpent called the devil, or Satan, who leads the whole world astray. He was hurled to the earth, and his angels with him.

ANGELS FORM HEAVEN'S CHOIR

There is one more thing angels do all day: angels praise God. The writers of the Psalms call upon the angels to worship God:

> Ascribe to the LORD, you heavenly beings,
> ascribe to the LORD glory and strength (Ps. 29:1).

> Let the heavens rejoice, let the earth be glad (Ps. 96:11).

> Praise the LORD from the heavens;
> praise him in the heights above.
> Praise him, all his angels;
> praise him, all his heavenly hosts (Ps. 148:1-2).

We see angels doing this on earth at the birth of Jesus. An angel tells the shepherds that the Messiah has been born in Bethlehem. 'Suddenly a great company of the heavenly host appeared with the angel, praising God and saying, "Glory to God in the highest heaven, and on earth peace to those on whom his favour rests"' (Luke 2:13-14).

But the primary location for their praise is heaven where they form the choirs of heaven. The seraphim in the prophet Isaiah's vision of God cry, 'Holy, holy, holy is the LORD Almighty; the whole earth is full of his glory' (Isa. 6:3). Isaiah describes them as 'calling to one another'. It's not explicitly said to be singing, though it is clearly a cry of praise and probably involves antiphonal singing (call and response). It's a cry echoed in Revelation 4:8 where the four living creatures cry: 'Holy, holy, holy is the Lord God Almighty, who was, and is, and is to come.'

In the final book of the Bible, the Apostle John is given a vision of heaven, and in his vision the angelic choirs often voice their praise of God. John, for example, sees Jesus, represented as a slain Lamb, opening the seals of a scroll which represents His authority to unfold God's purposes in history. After this, we read:

> Then I looked and heard the voice of many angels, numbering thousands upon thousands, and ten thousand times ten thousand. They encircled the throne and the living creatures and the elders. In a loud voice they were saying:
> 'Worthy is the Lamb, who was slain,
> to receive power and wealth and wisdom and strength
> and honour and glory and praise!' (Rev. 5:11-12).

We find a similar pattern in Revelation 7. The people of God sing the praises of Jesus the Lamb and the angels respond.

> All the angels were standing round the throne and round the elders and the four living creatures. They fell down on their faces before the throne and worshipped God, saying:

> 'Amen! Praise and glory
> and wisdom and thanks and honour
> and power and strength
> be to our God for ever and ever.
> Amen!' (Rev. 7:11-12).

Contrary to popular myth, we're also never told that angels play harps. It's the four living creatures, the twenty-four elders and the people of God who play harps in Revelation 5:8 and 15:2. In Revelation 14:2 we hear the sound 'like that of harpists playing their harps'. But it's not clear whether these are harps or harp-like music. And, if it is harp music, it's not clear who is playing, though the focus at this point is on the song sung by God's people rather than on the praise of angels.

In fact we're not even explicitly told that angels 'sing'. God's people are said to sing in heaven in the book of Revelation (14:1-3; 15:3-4). The four living creatures sing with the twenty-four elders in Revelation 5:9-10 and they may be a kind of angelic being. But generally the 'songs' of the angels are introduced with the words 'say' or 'saying' or 'shouting' (5:11-12, 13; 7:11-12; 11:15; 16:5-6; 19:1-3, 6-8). 'The adoration of the angels may be more of a chanted response than a hymn that is sung.'[9] Even the choir that appears over the skies of Bethlehem at the birth of Jesus is 'praising God and saying, "Glory to God …"' (Luke 2:13-14). It may be that, as spiritual beings without bodies (and therefore without voice boxes), the language of 'singing' is inappropriate for the music of angels. 'They have no need of tongue and hearing,' says John of Damascus, 'but without uttering words they communicate to

---

9. Robert H. Mounce, *The Book of Revelation,* New International Commentary on the New Testament, (Eerdmans, 1977), 149.

each other their own thoughts and councils.'[10] What is clear is that it is God's praises that angels proclaim and this is an act of worship.

SINGING WITH THE ANGELS

What's more, Hebrews 12 suggests there's a sense in which, when you gather to worship God in your local church, you join with the choirs of heaven.

> But you have come to Mount Zion, to the city of the living God, the heavenly Jerusalem. You have come to thousands upon thousands of angels in joyful assembly, to the church of the firstborn, whose names are written in heaven. You have come to God, the Judge of all, to the spirits of the righteous made perfect, to Jesus the mediator of a new covenant, and to the sprinkled blood that speaks a better word than the blood of Abel (Heb. 12:22-24).

Paul says, 'God raised us up with Christ and seated us with him in the heavenly realms in Christ Jesus' (Eph. 2:6). He's not talking about the future when Christ will unite heaven and earth. He's talking about now. We are united to Christ by faith through the work of the Holy Spirit. And, since Christ is before His Father in heaven, then in a sense so are we. Physically, of course, we remain on earth (you would have noticed if you had ascended into heaven!). But in terms of your identity and status you belong in heaven. Moreover, as Hebrews suggests, we enjoy a spiritual communion with Christ and therefore with the angels. We join together to praise God. The gathering of your

---

10. John of Damascus, *Exposition of the Orthodox Faith*, 2.3, in *The Nicene and Post-Nicene Fathers: Second Series,* Volume 2, eds. Philip Schaff & Henry Wace, 1899, reproduced (Hendrickson, 1994), 19.

church is like a portal to heaven. The vast gulf between heaven and earth becomes thin and porous when we meet around God's Word and sacraments. So there are angels standing next to you as you sing, and your praise mingles with theirs. A true Christian 'prays in the society of angels', wrote Clement of Alexandria at the end of the second century, 'and he is never out of their holy keeping; and though he pray alone, he has the choir of the saints standing with him.'[11]

---

11. Clement of Alexandria, 'The Stromata, or Miscellanies.' in *The Ante-Nicene Fathers,* Volume 2, ed. Alexander Roberts & James Donaldson, (Eerdmans, 1951), 545.

5.

Where do Angels lead us?

We've gained a picture of what angels are and the roles they perform. But what are we to do with this information? Where does this exploration of angels lead us? How are we to respond?

Much of what we know about angels is pieced together from the part they play in the story of salvation, and often their role is incidental to the main action. But there is one passage in the Bible that gives a sustained treatment to angels – Hebrews 1:1–2:4.

In the past God spoke to our ancestors through the prophets at many times and in various ways, but in these last days he has spoken to us by his Son, whom he appointed heir of all things, and through whom also he made the universe. The Son is the radiance of God's glory and the exact representation of his being, sustaining all things by his powerful word. After he had provided purification for sins, he sat down at the right

hand of the Majesty in heaven. So he became as much superior
to the angels as the name he has inherited is superior to theirs.
For to which of the angels did God ever say,

'You are my Son;

today I have become your Father'?

Or again,

'I will be his Father,

and he will be my Son'?

And again, when God brings his firstborn into the world,
he says,

'Let all God's angels worship him.'

In speaking of the angels he says,

'He makes his angels spirits,

and his servants flames of fire.'

But about the Son he says,

'Your throne, O God, will last for ever and ever;

a sceptre of justice will be the sceptre of your kingdom.

You have loved righteousness and hated wickedness;

therefore God, your God, has set you above your

companions by anointing you with the oil of joy.'

He also says,

'In the beginning, Lord, you laid the foundations
of the earth,

and the heavens are the work of your hands.

They will perish, but you remain;

they will all wear out like a garment.

You will roll them up like a robe;

like a garment they will be changed.

But you remain the same,

and your years will never end.'

To which of the angels did God ever say,

'Sit at my right hand until I make your enemies

a footstool for your feet'?

Are not all angels ministering spirits sent to serve those who will inherit salvation?

We must pay the most careful attention, therefore, to what we have heard, so that we do not drift away. For since the message spoken through angels was binding, and every violation and disobedience received its just punishment, how shall we escape if we ignore so great a salvation? This salvation, which was first announced by the Lord, was confirmed to us by those who heard him. God also testified to it by signs, wonders and various miracles, and by gifts of the Holy Spirit distributed according to his will.

The passage starts with Jesus. Jesus is God's ultimate word to humanity. In the past God spoke through dreams, visions and prophecies. But now He has spoken through His own Son (Heb. 1:1-2). Jesus is the Word made flesh, the ultimate revelation of God. Indeed, He is the exact representation of God's being (Heb. 1:3). If you want to know what God is like then look at Jesus. Jesus precisely reflects God's character because He is God. He is the radiance of God's glory (Heb. 1:3). God's glory is the perfection of His attributes and Jesus radiates those perfections. In Jesus we see the holiness, beauty, justice, love, power and wisdom of God. This means angelic appearances are less common today than during Bible times. 'Since the clear light of the gospel has arisen,' says Francis Turretin, and Jesus, 'the Lord of angels ... addresses us' – plus the Holy Spirit has been given to believers, and the canon of Scripture is complete – angelic messages have 'become less necessary'.[1]

---

1. Francis Turretin, *Institutes of Elenctic Theology, Volume One*, (P&R, 1992), 551.

Jesus is also the end of all things (as their heir) and the beginning of all things (as the One through whom they were made) (Heb. 1:2). And in between the beginning and end, Jesus sustains all things through His Word (Heb. 1:3). One of the big themes of the book of the Hebrews is the way Jesus purifies from sin both through His once-for-all sacrifice on the cross and through His permanent role as our heavenly priest. Here at the beginning of the letter, the writer trails this theme by saying: 'After he had provided purification for sins, he sat down at the right hand of the Majesty in heaven' (Heb. 1:3).

In verse 4 we are introduced to angels: 'So he became as much superior to the angels as the name he has inherited is superior to theirs.' Jesus is superior as the final Word, the only Son, the Creator and Sustainer, the ultimate sacrifice and the permanent priest. None of these are roles which angels can play. But why then does the writer say Jesus 'became' superior and that He 'inherited' a superior name? It's because, as the writer explains later, Jesus 'was made lower than the angels for a little while' (Heb. 2:9). Jesus is the eternal Son of God. In that sense He has always been superior to the angels. But at His incarnation He humbled Himself. He became human and human beings, as we've seen, are lesser beings than angels (Ps. 8:5; Heb. 2:7). Why did Jesus humble Himself in this way? 'So that by the grace of God he might taste death for everyone' (Heb. 2:9). Jesus came as a human being to die for human beings, to pay the death penalty our sin deserves in our place so that through faith we might be raised to glory.

FOLLOW THE AUTHORITY FROM ANGELS TO JESUS

The writer follows up his declaration that Jesus is superior to the angels with a series of quotes from the Old Testament to demonstrate and elaborate this truth. He begins with quotes from Psalm 2:7 and 2 Samuel 7:14:

> For to which of the angels did God ever say,
>
> > 'You are my Son;
> >
> > today I have become your Father'?
>
> Or again,
>
> > 'I will be his Father,
> >
> > and he will be my Son'? (Heb. 1:5).

At first glance, these might look like claims that, unlike the angels, Jesus has become the Son of God. The problem with this reading is that Jesus has always been God's Son. There wasn't a 'today' when Jesus first became God's Son. In fact these two quotes were both originally spoken to the human king of Israel. God promised to adopt the king as His quasi-son, thereby conferring some of His divine rule on the human king. So, in citing these two quotes, the writer of Hebrews is showing that Jesus is the ultimate King. God had promised that one of David's sons would always reign over God's people and Jesus is the fulfilment of that promise. The prophets had promised a coming Messiah. The word 'Messiah' literally means 'anointed one'. Rather than being crowned like modern monarchs, Israelite kings were anointed with oil. So the promise of a 'Messiah' or 'anointed one' was the promise of a king. 'Messiah' is a Hebrew word. The Greek equivalent is 'Christ'. So 'Christ' is not so much the name of Jesus as His job title.

This helps us understand the point the writer is making in Hebrews 1. Angels, as we've seen, are powerful beings who come in the name of God. When they act, they act with divine authority. But none of them has been given authority in their own right. Only Jesus is God's King. It is as God's King that

Jesus can send angels to do His bidding (Matt. 13:41-42; Rev. 22:16) and angels are described as belonging to Him, as 'his powerful angels' (2 Thess. 1:7). When we look at angels we are supposed to follow the lines of authority and be led to Jesus the ultimate King.

FOLLOW THE WORSHIP FROM ANGELS TO JESUS

Then the writer says:

And again, when God brings his firstborn into the world, he says,
'Let all God's angels worship him' (Heb. 1:6).

Angels feature heavily in the story of the birth of Jesus – as we know from school nativity plays. The angel Gabriel tells Zechariah that his wife will give birth to John the Baptist (Luke 1:11-20). It is Gabriel, too, who tells Mary she will conceive a child through the intervention of the Holy Spirit (Luke 1:26-38). An angel appears to Joseph to reassure him that Mary's pregnancy is a divine act (Matt. 1:20). A whole host of angels appears to the shepherds on the night Jesus is born, filling the skies with God's praises (Luke 2:8-15).

But every time the angels are pointing to Jesus. Imagine being on the hillside above Bethlehem when the skies were filled with angels. What a sight it must have been! But that was not the most amazing thing happening in Bethlehem that night. The real action, as the angel says, was 'lying in a manger' (Luke 2:12).

The point in Hebrews 1 is that worship is always offered by a lesser being to a greater being. Angels worship Jesus while Jesus never worships angels. It's a sure sign that Jesus is superior.

Indeed, angels get very upset if anyone tries to worship them! In the final book of the Bible John is given a vision of heaven and in this vision he is accompanied by an angelic guide. At one point John is so blown away by what he sees that he starts to worship the angel.

'I, John, am the one who heard and saw these things. And when I had heard and seen them, I fell down to worship at the feet of the angel who had been showing them to me. But he said to me, "Don't do that! I am a fellow servant with you and with your fellow prophets and with all who keep the words of this scroll. Worship God!"' (Rev. 22:8-9).

The angel is appalled by the idea that John might bow before him, and his response could not be clearer: 'Don't do that!' Angels may be more powerful than human beings, but there is only one division that really counts: between the Creator and His creation. And angels are on the same side of that division as human beings. So the Bible warns us not to be more interested in angels than the God who made them. The Apostle Paul warns against people who are obsessed with angels. He says they've lost connection with what really matters which is Jesus, the head of the church.

Do not let anyone who delights in false humility and the worship of angels disqualify you. Such a person also goes into great detail about what they have seen; they are puffed up with idle notions by their unspiritual mind. They have lost connection with the head, from whom the whole body, supported and held together by its ligaments and sinews, grows as God causes it to grow (Col. 2:18-19).

'The worship of angels' here is not a literal offering of worship to angels, argues N. T. Wright, but an ironic description of people who 'spend so much time in speculations about angels … that they are in effect worshipping them instead of God.'[2] The point is that to focus on angels is to miss the point! If you were to meet an angel, they might be bemused by your interest in them, and affronted by any adulation you offered them. If you asked them for help, they would reply, 'Why are you asking me? I'm only a servant. It's God you should be asking.' If you had an opportunity to ask them what they wanted you to do, they would say, 'Look to Jesus, worship Jesus, trust in Jesus, follow Jesus.' 'The angels,' says the third-century theologian Lactantius, 'do not want to be called gods and do not allow us to do this, because their one and only aim is to submit to God's will and to do only what he commands.'[3] John Calvin says:

> How preposterous it is for us to be led away from God by angels, who have been established to testify that his help is all the closer to us! But they do lead us away unless they lead us by the hand straight to him as our sole helper; unless we regard them as his hands that are moved to no work without his direction; unless they keep us in the one Mediator, Christ, that we may wholly depend upon him, lean upon him, be brought to him, and rest in him.[4]

---

2. N. T. Wright, *Colossians and Philemon*, Tyndale New Testament Commentaries, (IVP, 1986), 122.

3. Lactantius, *The Divine Institutes*, 2.17, cited in *Ancient Christian Doctrine Volume 1: We Believe in One God*, ed. Gerald L. Bray, (IVP, 2009), 133.

4. John Calvin, *The Institutes of Christian Religion*, Volume 1, trans. F.L. Battles, (Westminster Press/SCM, 1961), 1.14.12, 172.

We don't worship angels; instead we worship with angels. And together the One we worship is God the Father, Son and Spirit. As the liturgy of the Book of Common Prayer puts it:

> THEREFORE with Angels and Archangels, and with all the company of heaven, we laud and magnify thy glorious Name; evermore praising thee, and saying: Holy, holy, holy, Lord God of hosts, heaven and earth are full of thy glory: Glory be to thee, O Lord most High. Amen.[5]

If you get lost in the wild then one way of finding your way is to follow a river. Since gravity means water always flows downhill, then if you follow the flow of the river up-stream it will lead to high ground. The same is true with worship. If we follow the flow of worship it will lead to the high point. When we meet the worship of angels we're supposed to follow the flow, to give our attention to the One whom they are worshipping, and so be led to Jesus.

FOLLOW THE LIFE FROM ANGELS TO JESUS

In Hebrews 1:7 the writer says:

> In speaking of the angels he says,
> 'He makes his angels spirits,
> and his servants flames of fire.'

The idea seems to be that God gives to angels a temporary form as 'flames of fire', perhaps so they can appear to human beings. What is clear is that angels do not have life in themselves; they have existence only because God gives it to them. In this respect they are like human beings. The writer has already reminded us that Jesus sustains all things by His powerful word (Heb. 1:3).

---

5. From Holy Communion, The Book of Common Prayer (1662).

In contrast, the reign of Jesus will last forever (Heb. 1:8-9). There is nothing temporary about Jesus. That's looking forward. The writer also looks back: 'In the beginning, Lord, you laid the foundations of the earth, and the heavens are the work of your hands' (Heb. 1:10). Jesus was in the beginning. He Himself didn't have a beginning; instead He was the One who gave a beginning to everything else.

The other day I took one of my sweaters to my wife. 'I'm thinking of getting rid of this,' I said. 'Good!' she replied. 'Shall I just put it in the bin?' I asked. 'Well, no thrift shop is going to want it,' she exclaimed. There were holes at the elbows and the cuffs were frayed. But it's not just my clothes that wear out: I'm wearing out. My joints get achy, my muscles get tired and my memory isn't what it used to be (at least I don't think it's what it used to be). The whole of creation, says Hebrews 1:11-12, is wearing out like old clothes.

> They will perish, but you remain;
>> they will all wear out like a garment.
> You will roll them up like a robe;
>> like a garment they will be changed.

Today the writer might have spoken of entropy. Everything tends towards decay unless renewed by God. Nothing has life in itself – not even angels. Humans and angels alike depend for our existence on God. The one exception is Jesus. Jesus says:

> 'Very truly I tell you, a time is coming and has now come when the dead will hear the voice of the Son of God and those who hear will live. For as the Father has life in himself, so he has granted the Son also to have life in himself' (John 5:25-26).

Jesus has 'life in himself'. As a result, says Hebrews 1:12 (quoting Ps. 45:6-7), 'you remain the same, and your years will never end.' Another result of Jesus having life in Himself is that He's able to give eternal life to those who trust in Him. 'For just as the Father raises the dead and gives them life,' says Jesus, 'even so the Son gives life to whom he is pleased to give it' (John 5:21). We're to look at who is receiving life and who is giving life, and so be led to Jesus the Life-giver.

FOLLOW THE VICTORY FROM ANGELS TO JESUS

The writer's final Old Testament quote is from Psalm 110:1:

> To which of the angels did God ever say,
>   'Sit at my right hand
>   until I make your enemies
>   a footstool for your feet'? (Heb. 1:13).

The emphasis here is on the victory of Jesus. It's Jesus who has won the battle. He has sat down because His victory is complete. Now He simply waits for His victory to be consummated. The decisive action is over – done and dusted at the cross and resurrection. Jesus is the champion who has overcome the enemy. He took on death on our behalf and for three days death held Him in its icy grip. But on the third day Jesus rose victorious. 'Jesus Christ,' says 1 Peter 3:22, 'has gone into heaven and is at God's right hand – with angels, authorities and powers in submission to him.' Graham Cole says: 'The victorious Christ is now at the place of executive power at the right hand of God.'[6] Angels may be part of the

---

6. Graham A. Cole, *Against the Darkness*, (Crossway, 2019), 35.

army and indeed the Bible often portrays them in military terms as those who fight spiritual battles. But angels are just the foot soldiers; it's Jesus who is the Commander-in-Chief.

PAY ATTENTION

This comparison between Jesus and angels is all very interesting. But the writer has a deadly serious point to make. He continues:

> We must pay the most careful attention, therefore, to what we have heard, so that we do not drift away. For since the message spoken through angels was binding, and every violation and disobedience received its just punishment, how shall we escape if we ignore so great a salvation? This salvation, which was first announced by the Lord, was confirmed to us by those who heard him. God also testified to it by signs, wonders and various miracles, and by gifts of the Holy Spirit distributed according to his will (Heb. 2:1-4).

The point is this: we must pay attention to the message of Jesus. In fact, we're not simply to 'pay attention' to it, nor even 'careful attention'. We must pay 'the most careful attention' possible (Heb. 2:1).

The writer picks up the idea (an idea we've already noted) that angels were involved in delivering the Law of Moses (Deut. 33:2; Acts 7:38; Gal. 3:19). The involvement of angels added weight to the message of the law. But now the fulfilment of that message has come through Jesus. And, in all the different ways we've seen, Jesus is superior to angels. He is superior because unlike the angels He is truly God (as Hebrews chapter one demonstrates) and He is superior because unlike angels He became truly human to save His people (as Hebrews chapter two demonstrates). So if Jesus is superior then His message must be superior.

How important was the Law of Moses? Answer: very important. 'Every violation and disobedience received its just punishment,' says Hebrews 2:2. It was not a message to be trifled with. Yet the message of Jesus must be even more important because it was delivered by One who is superior to the messengers of the first message. With the coming of Jesus, the most important message received by humanity so far in history (the law of Moses) has now been fulfilled in a message (the message of Jesus) that is even more important.

This extended discussion of angels and the comparison to Jesus is all leading up to this point: the message of Jesus is super-important. Hence the need to pay it the most careful attention. 'How shall we escape if we ignore so great a salvation?' says Hebrews 2:3. The fact is there is no other escape route – at least none that works. Neither religious activity, nor good works provide an escape route because they can't rewind the clock and undo the sins we've committed against God. So Jesus said: 'I am the way and the truth and the life. No one comes to the Father except through me' (John 14:6).

In Hebrews 2:3 the writer says this message was 'first announced' by Jesus and then passed on by His first disciples ('those who heard him'). He's talking about what the Bible elsewhere calls 'the apostolic testimony' – the Spirit-inspired witness of the first apostles to Jesus. God confirmed their message through 'signs, wonders and various miracles' so we can be sure it's true (Heb. 2:4). Today we have that message—the message of salvation from Jesus, passed on by the apostles, and confirmed by the Holy Spirit—in the pages of the New Testament. God not only spoke through Jesus; He also ensured that future generations would have access to that message. There's every possibility you have a copy in your home. Maybe there's a copy of the Bible by your bedside. You will certainly have access to it through the internet.

Today we pay 'the most careful attention' to the message of Jesus by reading the New Testament and responding with faith. If you've not already done so, you might want to start by reading one of the four Gospels. As you do so, ask yourself: Who is Jesus? What has He come to do? And what does it mean to follow Him?

JESUS OVERCOMES SATAN BY EXPOSING HIS LIES

One important dimension of the message of Jesus is that He has overcome the evil angels. When He was on earth, Jesus said His exorcisms were a sign that He had come to conquer Satan (Matt. 12:28; Luke 10:17-20). He likened Satan to a strong man. Jesus was going to bind him so He could plunder his house (Matt. 12:29). This is what took place at the cross. Shortly before His crucifixion Jesus said: 'Now is the time for judgment on this world; now the prince of this world will be driven out' (John 12:31). Jesus has overcome Satan and is now releasing people from the power of Satan's grip through the mission of the church.

Jesus liberates people from Satan's grip by exposing Satan's lies. The first time we meet Satan in the Bible story he is lying (Gen. 3:1-7). In the Garden of Eden he portrayed God's rule as tyrannical. Adam and Eve, the first human beings, enjoyed a life of peace, plenty and protection under God's rule. But Satan, in the form of a serpent, implied that God was holding them back and they would be more free if they rejected God. In fact they ended up enslaved to sin and self, and cut off from the love, life and liberty of God. Yet ever since humanity has believed the lie that God is bad news and that we're better off without Him. Graham Cole calls Satan 'the great spoiler'.[7] Jesus says: '[The devil] was a murderer from the beginning, not holding to the truth, for there is no truth in him. When he lies, he speaks his native language, for he is a liar and the father of lies' (John 8:44). Paul says: 'The god of this age [Satan] has blinded the minds of unbelievers, so that they cannot see the light of the gospel that displays the glory of Christ, who is the image of God' (2 Cor. 4:4).

But Jesus has come as the Light to a world under the darkness of Satan's lies. He has come to refute those lies. Above all, He refutes the lie that God's rule is bad news. 'For even the Son of Man did not come to be served, but to serve,' He said, 'and to give his life as a ransom for many' (Mark 10:45). 'The Son of Man' was the way Jesus often referred to Himself. God's true King, Jesus, is not a king who takes, but a king who gives. He comes not with demands, but with grace.

Jesus is God's king coming to restore God's reign. That's good news because God's reign is a reign of love and life. But it's not good news for rebels. For rebels the re-imposition of God's rule is the bad news of defeat and judgment. But that aspect of God's rule is delayed. It will come when Christ returns, but not yet. Judgment did not fall when Christ first came to this earth. Or rather it did fall, but it fell on the King Himself in our place at the cross. Jesus took the judgment rebels deserve so we can be forgiven. It means those who seek refuge in Jesus can look forward to the final restoration of God's rule with joy.

---

7. Graham A. Cole, *Against the Darkness*, (Crossway, 2019), 26.

JESUS OVERCOMES SATAN BY
DISARMING HIS ACCUSATIONS

Jesus liberates people from Satan's grip by disarming Satan's accusations. Satan is the accuser (Zech. 3:1-5). This is his power: we have sinned against God and so we deserve God's judgment. In this sense we belong to Satan. We are destined to share his fate. His accusations get traction in our hearts because they reflect a truth – we really have sinned and we really do deserve God's judgment. But Jesus has disarmed the accusations of Satan. The Apostle Paul says:

> When you were dead in your sins and in the uncircumcision of your flesh, God made you alive with Christ. He forgave us all our sins, having cancelled the charge of our legal indebtedness, which stood against us and condemned us; he has taken it away, nailing it to the cross. And having disarmed the powers and authorities, he made a public spectacle of them, triumphing over them by the cross (Col. 2:13-15).

The law says we owe a debt to God (what Paul calls 'our legal indebtedness'). We have failed to obey Him as we should and so we owe reparations. Justice must be done. But it's a debt we can never repay and which therefore leaves us condemned. But Jesus has taken it away. The death penalty which the law demands has been paid by Him in full.

> Since the children have flesh and blood, he too shared in their humanity so that by his death he might break the power of him who holds the power of death – that is, the devil – and free those who all their lives were held in slavery by their fear of death (Heb. 2:14-15).

St Augustine writes:

While from the cross [the devil] received the power to slay the Lord's body outwardly, it was also from the cross that the inward power, by which he held us fast, was put to death. For it came to pass that the chains of many sins in many deaths were broken by the one death of the One who himself had no previous sin that would merit death. And, therefore, for our sake the Lord paid the tribute to death which was not his due, in order that the death which was due might not injure us … and therefore he openly exposed the principalities and the powers, confidently triumphing over them in himself.[8]

So Satan's accusations have no more traction. He has been disarmed. When Satan accuses, we can reply: 'Yes, you're right. I am a sinner and do deserve to be condemned. But Jesus has paid my debt. He has taken away my sin and given me His righteousness. He has removed my condemnation and shared with me the vindication of His resurrection. So away with you, Satan. Your words have no power here.'

It is a stance confirmed in heaven. Following the victory of the cross, Satan loses his place in heaven – the position from which he could make his accusations. Revelation 12:7-9 portrays this in graphic terms with Satan and his angels being thrown out of heaven by the other angels – like bouncers removing a troublesome guest. Then a loud voice declares:

'Now have come the salvation and the power
 and the kingdom of our God,
 and the authority of his Messiah.
For the accuser of our brothers and sisters [that is, Satan],

---

8. St Augustine, *On the Trinity*, 4.13.17; in Peter Gorday (eds.), *Colossians, 1-2 Thessalonians, 1-2 Timothy, Titus, Philemon,* Ancient Christian Commentary on Scripture: New Testament IX, (IVP, 2000), 36.

who accuses them before our God day and night,
    has been hurled down.
They triumphed over him
    by the blood of the Lamb
    and by the word of their testimony;
    they did not love their lives so much
    as to shrink from death' (Rev. 12:10-11).

The Apostle Paul puts it like this: 'I am convinced that neither death nor life, neither angels nor demons, neither the present nor the future, nor any powers, neither height nor depth, nor anything else in all creation, will be able to separate us from the love of God that is in Christ Jesus our Lord' (Rom. 8:38-39). Notice the inclusion of 'angels' and 'demons' in this list: neither angels nor demons can separate us from God's love in Christ. Jesus has disarmed Satan's accusations and He shares His victory with us if we have entrusted ourselves to Him. It is this that enables us to overcome the prince of darkness and his devils. The Reformer Martin Luther put it like this:[9]

And though this world, with devils filled,
Should threaten to undo us,
We will not fear, for God has willed
His truth to triumph through us.
The Prince of Darkness grim,
We tremble not for him;
His rage we can endure,
For lo! his doom is sure;
One little word shall fell him.

---

9. From 'A mighty fortress is our God', trans. Frederick H. Hedge.

Unseen Realities

Heaven, Hell, Angels and Demons

R. C. Sproul

The concept of the invisible spiritual realm is something which is difficult for us to grasp. What we can see, hear, and feel we can take on face value that it is reality. But what about those things that are unseen? Scripture speaks about heaven, hell, angels and demons which are a part of this invisible spiritual realm. Internationally renowned Bible teacher R. C. Sproul helps us gain an understanding of these things so that we can come to a realisation that in fact all four are true realities that impact upon our everyday lives.

ISBN 978-1-8455-0682-7

Christian Focus Publications

Our mission statement –

STAYING FAITHFUL

In dependence upon God we seek to impact the world through literature faithful to His infallible Word, the Bible. Our aim is to ensure that the Lord Jesus Christ is presented as the only hope to obtain forgiveness of sin, live a useful life and look forward to heaven with Him.

Our books are published in four imprints:

CHRISTIAN FOCUS

Popular works including biographies, commentaries, basic doctrine and Christian living.

CHRISTIAN HERITAGE

Books representing some of the best material from the rich heritage of the church.

MENTOR

Books written at a level suitable for Bible College and seminary students, pastors, and other serious readers. The imprint includes commentaries, doctrinal studies, examination of current issues and church history.

CF4•K

Children's books for quality Bible teaching and for all age groups: Sunday school curriculum, puzzle and activity books; personal and family devotional titles, biographies and inspirational stories – because you are never too young to know Jesus!

Christian Focus Publications Ltd,
Geanies House, Fearn, Ross-shire,
IV20 1TW, Scotland, United Kingdom.
www.christianfocus.com